T0178324

Lecture Notes of the Institute for Computer Sciences, Social Informatics and Telecommunications Engineering   447

More information about this series at https://link.springer.com/bookseries/8197

Yi-Bing Lin · Der-Jiunn Deng ·
Chao-Tung Yang (Eds.)

Smart Grid and Internet of Things

5th EAI International Conference, SGIoT 2021
Virtual Event, December 18–19, 2021
Proceedings

 Springer

Editors
Yi-Bing Lin
Department of Computer Science
National Chiao Tung University
Hsinchu, Taiwan

Der-Jiunn Deng
Department of Computer Science
and Information
National Changhua University of Education
Changhua City, Taiwan

Chao-Tung Yang
Department of Computer Science
Tunghai University
Taichung, Taiwan

ISSN 1867-8211   ISSN 1867-822X (electronic)
Lecture Notes of the Institute for Computer Sciences, Social Informatics
and Telecommunications Engineering
ISBN 978-3-031-20397-8   ISBN 978-3-031-20398-5 (eBook)
https://doi.org/10.1007/978-3-031-20398-5

This Springer imprint is published by the registered company Springer Nature Switzerland AG
The registered company address is: Gewerbestrasse 11, 6330 Cham, Switzerland

Preface

We are delighted to introduce the proceedings of the 5th edition of the European Alliance for Innovation (EAI) International Conference on Smart Grid and Internet of Things (SGIOT 2021), which took place at Windsor Hotel, Taichung, during December 18–19, 2021. This conference provided an opportunity for researchers, developers, and practitioners from around the world to connect and discuss recent findings in the area of the emerging smart grid and Internet of Things. The technical program of SGIOT 2021 consisted of 13 full papers in oral presentation sessions at the main conference tracks.

These technical papers cover a broad range of topics in wireless sensor, vehicular ad hoc networks, security, deep learning, and big data. Aside from the high-quality technical paper presentations, the technical program also featured three keynote speeches. The first keynote speech was entitled "Real-Time Multi-Robot Task Assignment in a Wireless Networked Smart Factory," by Kwang-Cheng Chen, from the University of South Florida, USA. The second keynote speech was entitled "Federated Learning through NOMA based gradient compression and through over the air computation," by Rose Hu, from Utah State University. The last keynote speech was entitled "Background, motivation, and performance of free5GC," by Jyh-Cheng Chen from the National Yang Ming Chiao Tung University, Taiwan.

Coordination with the steering chair, Imrich Chlamtac, was essential for the success of the conference. We sincerely appreciate his constant support and guidance. It was also a great pleasure to work with such an excellent organizing committee team for their hard work in organizing and supporting the conference. In particular, the Technical Program Committee, who completed the peer-review process for technical papers and helped to put together a high-quality technical program. We are also grateful to Conference Manager Carlos Valiente for his support and all the authors who submitted their papers to the SGIOT 2021 conference.

Yi-Bing Lin
Der-Jiunn Deng
Chao-Tung Yang
Chun-Cheng Lin
Rung-Shiang Cheng

Organization

Steering Committee

Imrich Chlamtac	University of Trento, Italy
Al-Sakib Khan Pathan	Independent University, Bangladesh
Der-Jiunn Deng	National Changhua University of Education, Taiwan

Organizing Committee

Honorary Chair

Pao-Tao Chen	Overseas Chinese University, Taiwan

General Chair

Yi-Bing Lin	National Yang Ming Chiao Tung University, Taiwan

General Co-chairs

Der-Jiunn Deng	National Changhua University of Education, Taiwan
Chao-Tung Yang	Tunghai University, Taiwan

Technical Program Committee Chair and Co-chairs

Chun-Cheng Lin	National Yang Ming Chiao Tung University, Taiwan
Rung-Shiang Cheng	Overseas Chinese University, Taiwan

Sponsorship and Exhibit Chair

Hui Hsin Chin	Overseas Chinese University, Taiwan

Local Chair

Rung-Shiang Cheng	Overseas Chinese University, Taiwan

Workshops Chair

Shao-Yu Lien   National Chung Cheng University, Taiwan

Publicity and Social Media Chair

Jen-En Huang   Overseas Chinese University, Taiwan

Publications Chair

Yu-Liang Liu   Overseas Chinese University, Taiwan

Web Chair

Chien-Liang Chen   Overseas Chinese University, Taiwan

Technical Program Committee

Chun-Cheng Lin   National Yang Ming Chiao Tung University,
                                      Taiwan
Rung-Shiang Cheng   Overseas Chinese University, Taiwan
Chien-Liang Chen   Overseas Chinese University, Taiwan
Yu-Liang Liu   Overseas Chinese University, Taiwan
Chang Li-Wei   Overseas Chinese University, Taiwan
Hung-Chang Chan   Overseas Chinese University, Taiwan
Jen-En Huang   Overseas Chinese University, Taiwan
Hui Hsin Chin   Overseas Chinese University, Taiwan

Contents

Applications on Internet of Things

Intellectual Property Protection of Zhuang Nationality Funeral Culture on Internet of Things

Min Ting Qin, Ying Huang, Yong Ming Chen, De Ying Wei, Zi Yi Wu, and Xiu Wen Ye[✉]

School of Politics and Law, Yulin Normal University, Yulin 537000, Guangxi, China
18677588510@qq.com

Abstract. The Zhuang nationality funeral culture is an important part of the ethnic culture in Guangxi Zhuang Autonomous Region, China. The Internet of Things can realize intelligent perception, recognition and management of objects through various information sensors and recognition technologies. With the development and popularity of the Internet of Things, the protection of intangible cultural heritage has gradually presented various forms and informationization, but this phenomenon has not been fully popularized nowadays, what's more, there is still a great lack of intellectual property protection for zhuang funeral culture under Internet of things technology. Digitalization of intangible cultural heritage has become an important trend in developing the intellectual property protection of intangible cultural heritage. Through literature analysis and quantitative research method, it is found that the application of Internet of Things technology in the protection of intangible cultural heritage in China is mainly reflected in information storage and publicity, and less intelligent management and identification of Internet of Things technology and the establishment of a complete database. Collecting and storing relevant data of the intangible cultural heritage about the funeral culture of the Zhuang nationality, and establishing the characteristic cultural information resource database of the intangible cultural heritage of the Zhuang nationality funeral will help to promote the digital protection of intellectual property of the Zhuang nationality funeral in China.

Keywords: The Internet of Things · Intangible cultural heritage · Intellectual property protection

1 Introduction

Intangible cultural heritage (hereinafter referred to as "intangible heritage") is an important symbol of the historical and cultural achievements in a country and a nation. Especially, it is and a vital part of excellent traditional cultures. Therefore, protecting and inheriting the intangible heritage of the nation can enhance national identity and cohesion. Even though China has adopted various methods to protect national cultures, the

Y.-B. Lin et al. (Eds.): SGIoT 2021, LNICST 447, pp. 3–12, 2022.
https://doi.org/10.1007/978-3-031-20398-5_1

traditional protection methods are unable to completely preserve the form of intangible cultural heritage and some important historical data, which may also lead to problems such as the confusion and lack of information about intangible cultural heritage. Through literature analysis and quantitative research method, it is found that the application of Internet of Things technology in the protection of intangible cultural heritage in China is mainly reflected in information storage and publicity, and less intelligent management and identification of Internet of Things technology and the establishment of a complete database. With the rapid development of the Internet. The market is growing, and the arrival of the era of big data, the means in protecting and inheriting China's intangible cultural heritage becomes diversified and informationized. How to make good use of the advantages of the big data era to protect, develop and inherit the Zhuang nationality funeral culture of Guangxi Zhuang Autonomous Region of China has become an urgent matter. In the era of big data, researching on the intellectual property protection of Guangxi Zhuang nationality funeral culture, not only can better protect and inherit this special funeral culture, reflect its patent value, copyright value and trademark value, but also can enhance the national spirit and provide a strong driving force for Zhuang funeral to apply for the intangible cultural heritage of humanity, besides, making a contribution for China's intangible heritage bank. Consequently, it is of practical significance to study the intellectual property protection of Zhuang nationality funeral culture in the era of big data by using the methods of literature analysis and quantitative research.

2   Literature Review of Intangible Cultural Heritage

In recent years, some traditional cultures in China have been slowly eliminated due to improper protection, so these traditional cultures urgently need to be protected thorough world cultural heritage application. At present, the protection of most intangible cultural heritages are mainly in traditional folk art and traditional architecture. However, the intellectual property protection and digital protection of intangible cultural heritage still need to be improved and developed. In the era of big data, it is very important to protect intangible cultural heritage through the means of intellectual property rights and digitalization. Some of the views on the study of intangible cultural heritage protection are summarized as follows:

2.1   Researches on the Intellectual Property Rights of the Intangible Cultural Heritage

Li Shunde (2006) affirmed the intellectual property rights protection of intangible cultural heritage, in addition, he proposed that special laws that are operable and targeted could be adopted in the protection. Qi Aimin (2007) and Jiang Yanli (2008) discussed some modes of the intellectual property rights protection in protecting the intangible cultural heritage, such as the patent rights protection, the copyright protection and the trademark rights protection. Mou Yanlin (2009) explored the approaches to provide intellectual property barriers and support for the protection of intangible cultural heritage. Gan Ming (2009) studied the rationality, legitimacy and inevitability lying in the intellectual property rights protection of intangible cultural heritage. Zhu Xianggui (2010) commented on the changes of legal mode in protecting the intellectual property rights of intangible cultural heritage. Zhou Anping (2009) and Zhiguo (2014) studied the present situation about the intellectual property rights protection of intangible cultural heritage worldwide, and they proposed that the intellectual property rights protection of intangible cultural heritage in China should adopt a comprehensive mode. Tan Dongli and Cao Xinming (2018) indicated to innovate the intellectual property rights protection of intangible cultural heritage in ethnic minorities, focusing on the intellectual property law.

2.2 Researches on the Digital Protection of Intangible Cultural Heritage

Peng Dongmei (2006) and Zhuo Mecuo (2013) put forward to conduct digital protection on folk art by using the digital information technology. Dong Yabo et al. (2011) show the effectiveness of Internet of Things technology in the protection of cultural sites. Ouyang Wenfeng (2013) pointed out that the Internet of Things technology should be applied to regional cultural construction to improve the construction and dissemination of culture. Wang Ting (2014) studied the Internet of Things technology in the protection of collections, enhanced its security and provided a new means of intelligent management of cultural relics. Shao Yan (2014) and Wang Mingyue (2015) pointed out that it was necessary to record, preserve and disseminate the intangible cultural heritage through digital and network technology. Song Lihua et al. (2015) analyzed the digital website of domestic intangible cultural heritage, and then she put forward the construction strategy and model of building the integration platform of intangible cultural heritage. Sun Chuanming et al. (2017) proposed that it was necessary to improve the digital system and mechanism for the intangible heritage of Guangxi ethnic minorities, so as to implement diversified digital means in the protection. Wang Long (2017) protected the intangible cultural heritage of Zhuang nationality funeral culture by making use of digital technology in the Internet era. Wang Weijie and Xiao Yuanping (2018) proposed to formulate a special development plan for the digital of intangible cultural heritage, so that gathering various forces to jointly build and share the intangible cultural heritage database of ethnic minorities. Gao Shan and Tan Guoxin (2020) studied the transformation of the intangible cultural heritage management paradigm under the driving force of big data. Wang Jingwu (2020) proposes to use Internet of things technology to carry out intelligent display and intelligent monitoring and management of ethnic folk museum, effectively protecting and spreading folk culture.

To sum up, some scholars have done a lot of researches on the intellectual property rights protection of intangible cultural heritage, mainly focusing on using the patent rights, copyright and trademark rights. As for the use of digital means to protect the intangible cultural heritage, relevant researches mainly focus on using digital network technology, all of these researches provide a basis for us to study the means in protecting the intangible cultural heritage, at the same time, it is more conducive to the protection and dissemination of intangible cultural heritage. However, as for the traditional etiquette protection of ethnic minorities, especially using the way of big data to protect Zhuang nationality funeral culture still needs further discussion. Using big data to protect the intellectual property rights of Zhuang nationality funeral culture is not only conducive to the inheritance of Zhuang nationality etiquette, but also beneficial to the protection of unique national and regional characteristics as well as the construction of a harmonious society. At the same time, it can improve the intangible heritage list system of China's ethnic minorities.

3 Analysis of the Intangible Cultural Heritage Problems

Intangible cultural heritage refers to all kinds of traditional cultural expressions handed down from generation to generation, which is regarded as an integral part of their cultural heritage. In addition, intangible cultural heritage also includes physical objects and places related to traditional cultural expressions. It is an important symbol of the historical and cultural achievements of a country and a nation, at the same time, it is an important part of excellent traditional culture. With the attention to the protection of intangible cultural heritage, there are more and more theoretical researches on intangible cultural heritage.

In the advanced search of academic journals on the official website of CNKI, when typing the topic of intangible cultural heritage and choosing the time period of 2002–2021, including the source categories of SCI, EI, CSSCI for retrieval, a total number of 223 qualified core journals were retrieved, but only 31 of them are related to intellectual property rights. There are only 5 articles on intellectual property rights from 2002 to 2008, 19 articles from 2009 to 2015 and 7 articles from 2016 to 2021 (see Fig. 1). From the findings, it can be known that the number of core journals about intellectual property rights in all of the core journals about intangible cultural heritage at each stage is relatively less. It presents that in the intangible cultural heritage research, there is less researches on protecting the intangible cultural heritage through intellectual property rights. However, there is great significance to protect the intangible cultural heritage through intellectual property rights. China Court Network pointed out that the intellectual property rights system as the first choice of private power to protect the intangible cultural heritage is difficult to shake and indispensable. Moreover, Li Shunde (2006) affirmed the intellectual property rights protection of intangible cultural heritage. Theoretical research is the forerunner of practice, so the lack of theoretical research on the protection of intangible cultural heritage through intellectual property rights will affect relevant protection. How to promote the development of intangible cultural heritage through the patent law, trademark law and copyright law provided in the intellectual property rights law is a problem to be thought about and studied nowadays. At the same time, the funeral culture of Zhuang nationality is also an excellent traditional culture passed down by the Zhuang nationality from generation to generation, so the intellectual property rights can be utilized to promote the funeral culture of Zhuang nationality to become an intangible cultural heritage.

For According to the data released on the China Intangible Cultural Heritage Network, 42 projects in China have been included in the intangible cultural heritage list by the United Nations Educational Scientific and Cultural Organization (UNESCO), ranking first in the world. There are a total of 1,557 national representative items of intangible cultural heritage in the China's intangible culture list, with a total of 3,610 sub-items according to the declared areas or units. In the classification view of intangible cultural heritage, we found that folk category of intangible cultural heritage accounted for 492, which is 14% of the total amount (see Fig. 2). Taking a general view of the

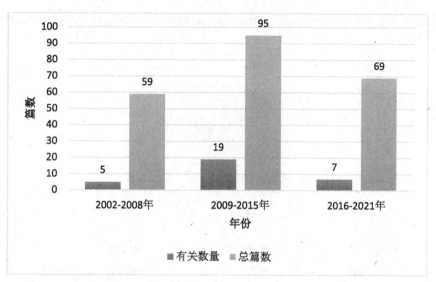

Fig. 1. Number of articles on intellectual property rights in the intangible cultural. number heritage documents during 2002–2021. Cultural number data source: sorted out by the researcher

proportion taken by all representative categories in China's national intangible cultural heritage, it is found that the proportion of folk category is not low. Therefore, it can be concluded that, firstly, it affirms the value of folk intangible cultural heritage. Some folk customs such as the Spring Festival, the Dragon Boat Festival, the March 3rd of Zhuang nationality, Zhuang nationality song fair, etc. are listed as the national intangible cultural heritages, which is the affirmation of these excellent traditional cultures as well as the protection and inheritance of them. Secondly, the folk intangible cultural heritage is not comprehensive. In China's national intangible culture heritage list, there are only 43 projects related to the etiquette customs in folk category, let alone the project about funeral. But the funeral culture also is significant in research and protection. For example, researching and protect the Zhuang nationality funeral culture is conducive to the protection of ethnic minority culture, thus making the inheritance of some excellent national culture becomes possible; besides, it is also conducive to human's excavation and protection of intangible cultural heritage. In the era of big data, the collection and storage of information has become simple and convenient, but the excavation and protection of Zhuang nationality funeral culture is not only relying on rigid data. Under the application of the Internet of things technology, through all kinds of possible Internet access, form a new way of cultural transmission, zhuang funeral and non-material cultural heritage content and content in the connection, between the zhuang funeral with man and intangible cultural heritage and the pan in the connection, realize the intelligent perception, recognition and management of zhuang nationality funeral. How to promote the protection and excavation of Zhuang nationality funeral culture by using big data, and even to promote the development of intangible cultural heritage in China, is a problem to be considered and studied today. How to use big data to promote the protection of the excavation of the Zhuang funeral, and even promote the development of

Chinese intangible cultural heritage, is a major problem to be thought about and studied nowadays.

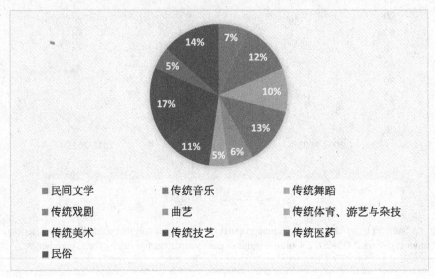

Fig. 2. Representative list of China's national intangible cultural heritage. Data source: sorted out by the researcher

In the official website of Law Credit of China, when typing the key words of mourning, funeral, bury, tomb and grave for finding relevant literature, it is found that the number of mourning literature is 327, the number of bury literature is 633, the number of funeral literature is 194, the number of tomb literature is 1,210, the number of grave literature is 54, with the total number of 2,418 (see Fig. 3). Based on the analysis of these data, it is concluded that, firstly, there are a large number of documents about mourning, funeral, bury, tomb and grave, indicating that they have been widely concerned by people, and they also have great value in research and protection. Secondly, the feasibility of protecting Zhuang nationality funeral culture through the intellectual property rights. There are a number of 194 documents on funeral culture, which indicates that some predecessors had adopted intellectual property rights to explore and protect the funeral culture, so that proving the feasibility of using intellectual property rights to protect Zhuang nationality funeral. However, on the other hand, the number of documents on funeral is relatively small. There is still a long way to go to explore and protect the funeral culture of the Zhuang nationality through using the intellectual property rights. At present, how to explore the value of Zhuang nationality funeral culture through the bridge of intellectual property and make use of its cultural value is a problem to be thought about and studied.

In the era of big data, how to explore and protect the Zhuang nationality funeral culture through big data? How to play the role of patent, trademark and copyright of intellectual property rights in the Zhuang nationality funeral culture? How to promote the development of intangible cultural heritage by using the intellectual property rights?

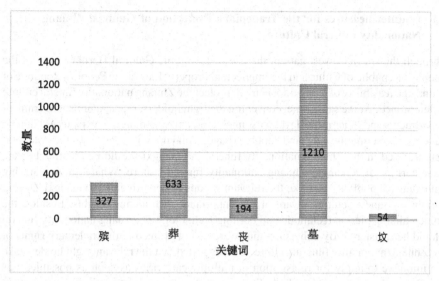

Fig. 3. Number of relevant documents on "Mourning", "Funeral", "Bury", "Tomb" and "Grave". Data source: sorted out by the researcher

Conducting researches on these questions is helpful to promote the further development of Zhuang nationality funeral culture, so as to make it show the value in the new era. In addition, these researches are beneficial to promote the Zhuang nationality funeral culture to become a national intangible cultural heritage, so that enhancing the intangible cultural heritage to coruscate new vitality in the new era.

4   Countermeasures for Intellectual Property Protection of Zhuang Nationality Funeral Culture

The "tradition" of national traditional culture is a dynamic cultural entity, which is not rigid or constant. Intangible cultural heritage cannot be stored or protected only by traditional stereotype. So the means for protecting traditional national culture should not be single, but diversified, multi-faceted and all-round. With the development of economy, we have ushered in the era of big data. At present, 42 projects in China have been listed by UNESCO on the list of intangible cultural heritage, ranking first in the world. Therefore, we should make good use of the thinking of big data, technology and resources, so as to protect, inherit and develop our traditional national culture. However, there are still many ethnic cultures in China that have not been well protected, such as "Guangxi Zhuang nationality funeral culture", especially in the current era of big data, we should pay more attention to the protection of the intellectual property rights of Guangxi Zhuang nationality funeral culture.

4.1 Countermeasures for the Trademark Protection of Guangxi Zhuang Nationality Funeral Culture

Through the special investigation, the use of Intangible Cultural Heritage Law of the People's Republic of China and the Intellectual Property Law of the People's Republic of China, the feasibility of using trademark to protect the Zhuang nationality funeral culture is determined. At the same time, convening the right holders, relevant units, government departments and other multi-level personnel to organize seminars. The patterns "double phoenixes greeting the sun" and "double dragons playing with a peal" on the gold altar that are used in the Zhuang nationality funeral in Guangxi should be identified as the trademark of the Guangxi Zhuang nationality funeral culture. What's more, carrying out extensive publicity to make the relevant groups or departments of Guangxi Zhuang nationality funeral culture aware of the importance of trademark rights. Besides, the golden altar depiction technique and burning technology of Zhuang nationality funeral should be registered. By enhancing the awareness of protecting the trademark rights of the Zhuang nationality funeral culture, it is suggested that the relevant right holders take the initiative to apply for registration in multiple categories as soon as possible, thus mobilizing the people of the whole Zhuang autonomous region to actively participate in the protection work of Zhuang nationality funeral. Through the efforts of all the people in Guangxi to support the protection of Guangxi Zhuang nationality funeral culture.

4.2 Countermeasures for the Copyright Protection of Guangxi Zhuang Nationality Funeral Culture

Copyright protects original literary works. There are many similarities between the "mourning songs" of Guangxi Zhuang nationality funeral and ordinary works. For example, both of them are works of human thoughts and labors, which should be expressed in a certain form (written, oral, etc.), and they are spread in a similar way. Hence, relevant provisions of copyright can be adopted to protect the literature about Guangxi Zhuang nationality funeral culture. In order to prevent others from using or adapting the "morning songs" of Guangxi Zhuang nationality funeral without the consent of right holders, so as to protect the inheritance integrity of literary works about Guangxi Zhuang nationality funeral culture and protect the legitimate rights and interests of relevant right holders.

4.3 Countermeasures for Protecting Guangxi Zhuang Nationality Funeral Culture by Using the Big Data

The massive storage of information and intelligent choreography technology of big data are used to systematically summarize the mourning songs of the Zhuang nationality funeral culture, and show them to the public according to the characteristic languages of different areas of Zhuang nationality. In this way, it can not only make the mourning custom of the Zhuang nationality be well inherited and protected, but also make the custom be innovative and developed during the process of constantly adapting to the social development. Vigorously promoting the integration and innovation between Zhuang nationality funeral culture and big data technology, in addition, using and developing digital protection technology of intangible cultural heritage. By using the Internet of things technology to collect information about zhuang funeral utensils, data analysis and protection measures are made to prevent the loss of utensils due to the lack of inheritors. Collecting and recording the artifacts used in the funeral of Zhuang nationality firstly, so as to prevent the loss of some kinds of artifacts due to the lack of inheritors. Then, different digital protection technologies are adopted according to the funeral rituals and customs of different areas and different nationalities of the Guangxi Zhuang autonomous region. These resources of funeral rituals as well as customs are digitized and visualized by using modern virtual reality technology, new media technology and digital technology, and then realizing classified storage, accurate retrieval, rapid transmission and real-time sharing gradually, so as to make the digital resources of Zhuang nationality funeral culture knowledgeable and easy to use. Through the network communication technology to design and construct web pages with the theme of Zhuang nationality funeral culture, and adding rich pictures, audios, videos and other resources. What's more, gathering various forces to create the Guangxi Zhuang nationality funeral database, so that making sure the customs of Zhuang nationality funeral culture can be well protected and spread to the public.

5 Conclusion

As an important part of the characteristics in Guangxi folk customs, the funeral custom of the Guangxi Zhuang Autonomous Region is also a valuable treasure of the traditional Chinese culture, which are of great research value and inheritance significance. With the increasingly rapid pace of social reform and renewal of the environment, the funeral custom of Guangxi Zhuang nationality is facing many problems in development, such as the imperfect inheritance and lack of information, etc. At present, in the era of big data, to explore the combined use of intellectual property rights and big data, to inherit and protect Zhuang nationality funeral culture through patent rights, trademarks and copyrights in the intellectual property rights, at the same time, combining the digital, scientific and technological means to carry forward and innovate the funeral culture of Zhuang nationality is an important way to protect the Zhuang nationality funeral culture. But through carrying out the data research, it is found that China is still in a missing state in the field of combining intellectual property rights with big data to protect the Zhuang nationality funeral culture, so it can be seen that the protection of funeral culture of the Zhuang nationality still has a long way to go. How to make practical use of intellectual property rights and big data to achieve the protection and inheritance of Zhuang nationality funeral culture has become an urgent need to solve. Under the framework of the theoretical system studied and discussed by scholars, departments from multiple sectors need to give full play to the practical protection of Zhuang nationality funeral culture in the future, so as to construct a good development of theoretical research and practical implementation, and to better push ahead the good inheritance and development of Zhuang nationality funeral culture.

Acknowledgments. This work was supported by the Research Center for cultural construction and social governance in ethnic areas of Yulin Normal University (2019YJJD0003).

References

Dongyabo, Z.B., ludongming, F.: Research and application of Internet of things technology for the protection of cultural sites. Cult. relics Prot. Archaeol. Sci. **23**(3), 75–78 (2011)

Gan Ming, F., Liu Guangzi, S.: Study on the feasibility of intellectual property protection of intangible cultural heritage law. Acad. Forum, 9–12 (2009)

Gao Shan, F., Tan Guoxin, S.: Research on the transformation of intangible cultural heritage management paradigm driven by big data. Libr. Spec. Stud. **11**, 76–82 (2020)

Li Shunde, F.: Intellectual property protection of national cultural heritage. Jiangxi Soc. Sci. 7–12 (2006)

Li Ziran, F.: Discussion on the nature, characteristics, protection and development of traditional national culture. Heilongjiang Natl. Ser. **1**, 103 (2006)

Mou Yanlin, F.: Intangible cultural heritage protection-from the perspective of intellectual property. Ethn. Art Stud. 4–48 (2009)

Ouyang Wenfeng, F.: The positive significance of the development of the Internet of things to regional cultural communication – a case study of Hunan. Acad. Forum 176–182 (2013)

Peng Dongmei, F.: Digital protection-a new way of intangible cultural heritage protection. Cult. Heritage 47–51 (2006)

Qi Aimin, F.: Basic legal issues concerning the protection of intangible cultural heritage. Acad. Stud. 22–25 (2007)

Shao Yan, F.: Research on copyright law issues in the digitization of intangible cultural heritage. Study Ethnics Guangxi **5**, 163–168 (2014)

Song Lihua, F., Li Wanshe, S., Dong Tao, T.: Digital protection of intangible cultural heritage and construction of knowledge integration platform. Libr. J. **1**, 73–81 (2015)

Sun Chuanming, F., Cheng Qiang, S., Tan Guoxin, T.: Analysis on the present situation and countermeasures of digital protection of intangible cultural heritage in Guangxi ethnic minorities. Study Ethnics Guangxi **3**, 124–132 (2017)

Tan Dongli, F., Cao Xinming, S.: Research on intellectual property protection of intangible cultural heritage of ethnic minorities. Guizhou Ethn. Stud. **2**(39), 38–42 (2018)

Tian Shengbin, F., Lan Nan, S., Jiang Yanli, T.: Legal thinking on the protection of intangible cultural heritage from the perspective of intellectual property. Hubei Soc. Sci. **2**, 148–151 (2008)

Wang Ting, F.: Application analysis of Internet of things technology in museum collection management – Taking Qinshihuang Mausoleum Museum as an example. Cult. relics Prot. Archaeol. Sci. **26**(1), 94–98 (2014)

Wang Long, F.: Digitalization of the intangible cultural heritage in the era of "Internet+". Seeker 193–197 (2017)

Wang Mingyue, F.: Reflection on digital risk and path of intangible cultural heritage protection. Cult. Heritage **3**, 32–40 (2015)

Wang Weijie, F., Xiao Yuanping, S.: Present situation and development countermeasures of the digital protection of intangible cultural heritage of ethnic minorities in Guizhou. J. Hubei Univ. Nationalities **36**(4), 120–123 (2018)

Wang Jingwu, F.: Research on museum informatization and intelligent service mode based on internet of things technology. Inform. Sci. 45–50 (2020)

Zhi Guo, F.: Discussion on the intellectual property protection of intangible cultural heritage. Guangxi Soc. Sci. **7**(229), 180–183 (2014)

Zhou Anping, F., Chen Yun, S.: Selection of intellectual property protection mode of intangible cultural heritage under the perspective of international law. Acad. Forum **19**(109), 3–9 (2009)

Zhu Xianggui, F.: International law protection of educational autonomy of intangible cultural heritage of ethnic minorities. Ethn. Educ. Study **2**(21), 30–34 (2010)

Zhuo Mecuo, F.: Research on the digital protection of intangible cultural heritage. Res. Explor. Lab. **32**(8), 226–248 (2013)

China IoT UBI Car Insurance Regulatory Development Trend

Xiu Wen Ye, Ying Huang$^{(\boxtimes)}$, Min Ting Qin, and Xiao Ying Huang

Law, Yulin Normal University, Yulin 537000, Guangxi, China
2806422184@qq.com

Abstract. The innovation of China's electronic information technology has promoted the birth and development of the new IoT UBI auto insurance in China. IoT UBI auto insurance based on the Internet of things shows the unique functions and advantages of multi-dimensional construction and development, also put forward important requirements for China's multi-faceted supervision, among which the unstable external environment determines that IoT UBI needs stricter and more cautious supervision. Through literature analysis and quantitative analysis, it is found that the Chinese government lacks clear regulations, regulatory policies, and regulatory support for IoT UBI. Based on the lack of national supervision procedures and the difficulty in building the system, it is necessary to establish relevant supervision procedures and future corresponding policies and regulations to provide legal support for national supervision departments, to promote the supervision of IoT UBI in China to be more inclusive and comprehensive.

Keywords: Internet of things · UBI auto insurance · Government supervision · Big data

1 Introduction

As a new type of auto insurance developed gradually in China, UBI (Usage-based insurance) has ushered in a higher development stage with the continuous enhancement of China's Internet and electronic technology. Nowadays, some electronic information technology companies in China have developed IoT UBI-related products and businesses, such as IoT UBI hardware boxes, mobile phone software connected with customers, and systems providing digital computing, etc., which provide more perfect technical support for the formal development of IoT UBI. The development trend of IoT UBI is more inclined to the system development of scientific and technological products and insurance institutions. Via the matching of IoT UBI products developed by technology companies and IoT UBI of insurance institutions, more accurate IoT UBI policies are developed, which has greater technological innovation and digital development. However, it is based on the digital characteristics of IoT UBI, which collects a large amount of customer information for calculation, but also has potential safety hazards of excessive collection, disclosure and dissemination of customer information. Customers' privacy rights will be virtually violated. IoT UBI itself has powerful functions and multi-dimensional development characteristics, which involve a wide range of industries, so China has not yet built a perfect supervision system. This paper studies China's IoT UBI industry and its regulatory documents and relevant laws and regulations literature analysis and quantitative analysis, hoping to predict the development trend of China's IoT UBI regulation in the future from scientific evidence. Promote the steady and long-term development of IoT UBI auto insurance in China.

2 Introduction

China has become the fastest-growing country in the world with the continuous development of the economy. automobile insurance has become a major type of insurance in China due to the increase of national per capita income and automobile ownership. In the era of big data, the auto insurance industry gave birth to UBI with the rapid development of IOV. China's UBI is still in its infancy and has not been fully popularized so that there are few articles on UBI, which mainly focus on three aspects: driving behavior, risk assessment & building-related data models of UBI, and difficulties faced by China in developing UBI.

2.1 Research on Driving Behavior

Dai Jianguo (2015) pointed out that introducing UBI as additional insurance can reduce the information asymmetry in the auto insurance market. We should focus on the principle of balance between driving behavior insurance and consideration in the future and fundamentally solve the problems such as car-hailing service insurance by technical path, according to Han Changyin (2020). Zhang Haixia (2020) studied the necessity of intelligent IOV based on vehicle behavior analysis. Wu Xiangyou (2020) believed that the UBI pricing model based on driving behavior can reflect driving risk more truly.

2.2 Research on Risk Assessment of UBI and Construction of Related Data Model

Wang Li (2017) collected and processed vehicle behavior data, analyzed periodic behavior UBI, and built a preliminary risk model. Li Siyao (2017) studied the current process of UBI in China and the current situation of UBI-based auto insurance pricing model and pointed out that there is a lack of environmental factors in UBI risk factors at present. Liu Jian (2019) developed a reasonable UBI rate model for commercial vehicles based on the construction of the UBI big data analysis model and UBI big data analysis model of IOV.

2.3 Research on the Dilemma of UBI in China

Dai Jianguo (2015) believed that the promotion of UBI in China faces the inaccuracy of risk classification variables and the lag of national insurance policies. Zhu Jiazhen (2020) pointed out that the operation of UBI is still faced with the conflict between UBI and the rules of disclosure obligation, with distortion risks and potential safety hazards of data. Jiang Yu (2020) believed that the promotion of UBI in China still faces the dilemmas that large insurance companies lack the motivation to develop UBI, too much investment in UB in the early stage, insufficient data analysis technology and privacy of user data. Sun Hongtao (2020) believed that although the development of UBI in China solves the problem of car-hailing service insurance, it still needs the unification of technical standards and the improvement of the supervision system. Shao Chengyin (2018) pointed out that it is difficult to establish an accurate actuarial model in China's UBI operation mode, the product quality and service quality are imperfect, and the personal information of users is easy to be leaked without knowing it.

To sum up, some scholars have studied driving behavior to meet the need to collect various data of drivers' driving behavior when developing UBI, so that accurate and personalized premium standards can be formulated; Studying the risk assessment of UBI and constructing relevant data model can provide the corresponding reference for insurance institutions when formulating personalized premiums; Studying the dilemma of developing UBI in China is beneficial to grasp the current situation of UBI development in China, and to learn experience for the optimal development of UBI. However, deficiencies still exist in the supervision system and development trend of UBI in China. Studying the development trend of UBI supervision in China will fill the deficiencies in system supervision and optimize the development environment of UBI, which is beneficial to the popularization of UBI in China.

3 Analysis of UBI in China

3.1 History of UBI in China

When UBI auto insurance became popular in European and American countries, some insurance and technology companies in China paid attention to this innovative auto insurance product, among which many well-known insurance companies and high-end information and electronic technology companies explored and tested together to build a UBI auto insurance development model combining insurance companies with technology companies, and achieved ideal results.

According to the representative achievements of development achievements, we select two insurance companies for demonstration research. PICC participated in many UBI research projects from 2016 to 2020, that is, in 2016, it cooperated to design the application of UBI premiums and jointly launched the research on data collection standards of car networking and the calculation of risk factors; In 2018, UBI passed the innovation product review of insurance organizations, and PICC was allowed to operate UBI products during the pilot period of independent pricing reform; In 2019, the automobile physical damage insurance clauses on UBI were released; In 2020, it signed a UBI contract with Business Car Cloud (Fig. 1). China Life Insurance Company developed a UBI data detection system with Rongzhi's car networking interconnection in 2015, and it reached a partnership with Changan Auchan and Shanghai Pingjia Network Technology Co., Ltd. to develop and promote UBI insurance business in 2016 (see Fig. 2). The combination system of insurance and technology has bridged a lot for the development of UBI in China. Through the study of these two demonstration systems of the combination of insurance and technology, it is found that this combination development system has also achieved more benefits and achievements in the market development, which has achieved an exemplary role in the construction of the development system of UBI in China.

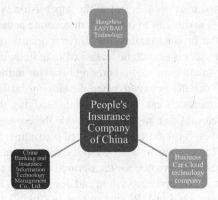

Fig. 1. UBI by People's Insurance Company of China. Data from: Researchers Data Collation

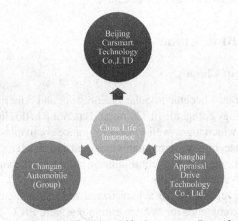

Fig. 2. UBI Relationship Diagram of China Life Insurance. Data from: Researchers Data Collation

3.2 UBI Technology in China

Driven by "Internet+" and scientific & technological innovation, "Insurance + Technology" has become a new development trend of the insurance industry and formed a new industry term "Insurance Technology". Insurance technology relies on the Internet platform to apply big data, cloud computing, and artificial intelligence technologies to the company's operation and insurance business development, to improve business efficiency and change product form by infiltrating the whole process of the insurance business. Then, the way of service and interaction with customers is improved to give birth to a new business model and construct a new insurance ecology (Ren Yuan 2019).

Since UBI entered the Chinese market, many technology companies have actively carried out research and development of UBI's data monitoring system, intelligent calculation, user operation procedures, and other data and technologies, that is, using big data technology to collect users' driving static and dynamic information to establish a preliminary image system, which achieves research results in many fields. Some companies have realized the combination of hardware and software of computer systems to collect and process information and preliminarily calculate the driver's image system. The main business and product information of the following enterprises are inquired through the official system of Tianyancha, such as AUTO Software and AUTO Box of Beijing Carsmart Technology, TBOX Products, Didihu AI IOV Service System and Jiabao Box of Shenzhen Guanglian Saixun, PC Management Software LASO of Jiangnan Digital DNA Technology and GID Series of Intelligent Vehicle Terminal. Nanjing Renren Insurance's Chebao APP and Shanghai Appraisal Drive Technology Co., Ltd.'s Appraisal Baobao APP need to be used together with other hardware products to feedback the data to the platform; ICC of Shenzhen Yuanzheng Technology and the NICEGO of Hangzhou NICEGO Technology are hardware products that can quickly feedback data to the platform in real-time without being used with other software (see Table 1). Under the in-depth research and active exploration of many Chinese technology companies, UBI products in China and even in the world are richer, more complete, and diversified.

Table 1. .

– Company name	– Major business	– Representative UBI products	
		– Hardware	– System software
– Beijing Carsmart Technology Co., LTD	– Committed to the development of the IOV, IoT, and the Beidou industry	– AUTO Box, TBOX products, wireless driving recorder, VANET	– YangCheBao, CheDainTong, AUTO
– Nanjing Renrenbao Network Technology Co., Ltd	– Construct posture data and driving risk technology algorithm and turn it into a UBI business model of safe driving income through safe driving behavior	–	– Chebao

(continued)

Table 1. (*continued*)

– Company name	– Major business	– Representative UBI products	
		– Hardware	– System software
– Shenzhen Yuanzheng Technology Co., Ltd	– Develop R&D, production and sales of high-end automobile diagnosis, testing and maintenance products	– TBOX terminal (passenger car, commercial vehicle), ICC	–
– Shenzhen Guanglian Saixun Co., Ltd	– Provide SAAS platform and its data operation services for customers in different vertical industries with technologies such as IOV big data algorithm and artificial intelligence as the core	– Che Yunbao, WeChat Platform, DD BOX and Jiabao Box	– DidiHu AI IOV Service System
– Shanghai Appraisal Drive Technology Co., Ltd	– Focus on user behavior big data and independently develop UBI algorithm model based on driving behavior risk assessment	–	– Appraisal Baobao
– Jiangsu Digital DNA Technology Co., Ltd	– IOV solution provider, focusing on vehicle digital gene technology and creating the original technology of "Cloud & Pipeline & Terminal" architecture	– Intelligent vehicle terminal GID series, Driving images	– PC-side management software LASO
– Hangzhou NICEGO Technology Co., Ltd	– UBI Automotive Big Data Company based on ADAS adheres to the new model of two-wheel drive and focuses on the first stage industrialization of unmanned driving	– NICEGO	–

Data from: Researchers Data Collation.

In the era of big data, "Big Data + Insurance" is the inevitable development trend of the insurance business and big data provides preconditions for the mature development of IoT UBI. In the era of data sharing and circulation, the leakage of private information has become a common development problem. IoT UBI's data all rely on big data, so the problem that users' private information is illegally leaked and sold is more prominent. The adverse effects not only harm the interests of individuals and society but also will inevitably bring great obstacles to the rapid development of IoT UBI.

3.3 China IoT UBI Car Insurance System

After The unique tagging nature of RFID gives the IoT the characteristic of traceability, which in UBI makes it possible to keep track of the exact location of a vehicle and its surroundings. The M2M system framework is a core, networked application, and service with intelligent interaction of machine terminals that will enable intelligent control of objects. Based on the cloud computing platform and intelligent network, insurance companies can make decisions based on the data obtained from the sensor network, change the behavior of IoT UBI car insurance objects for control and feedback so that users can correct their bad behavior, report the vehicle's driving situation, their driving behavior and other information to the vehicle owner. Cloud computing can reduce the processing burden of the user terminal by continuously improving the " cloud " processing capacity, eventually simplifying it into a simple input and output device, and enjoying the powerful computing and processing capacity of the "cloud" on demand.IoT UBI car insurance obtains a large amount of data information through the IoT sensing layer. After transmission through the network layer, it is put on an insurance platform and then processed by a high-performance application layer to give these data intelligence in order to be finally converted into useful information for end-users. The sensor network is a vast network of sensors formed by micro-electro-mechanical systems (MEMS), giving ordinary objects a new life, giving them their data transmission pathways, storage functions, operating systems, and specialized applications. This allows the IoT to monitor and protect people through objects, and IoT UBI car insurance has the dual function of monitoring the safety and protection of car owners (see Fig. 3).

3.4 CHina's Auto Insurance Laws and Regulations

In China's auto insurance industry, it is not uncommon for enterprise personnel to illegally sell and disclose users' private information. UBI, a new type of insurance-related regulations system is not perfect, so this kind of phenomenon is more prominent, calling for reasonable and effective management methods. The action of protecting users' privacy needs users to improve their awareness of privacy information protection, and it also needs the solid strength of the government to supervise and standardize the auto insurance industry to promote the good development of UBI in China.

After sorting out and summarizing in PKULAW.com, it is concluded that the Chinese government's supervision of the auto insurance market has been going on for a long time, that is, since 2000, there have been relevant laws and regulations to supervise the auto insurance market. From only central regulations to adding local regulations and industry

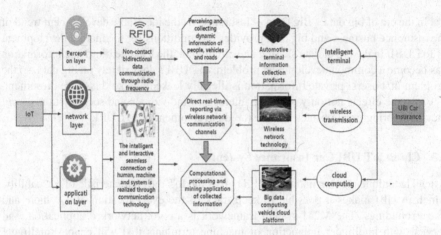

Fig. 3. China IoT UBI Car Insurance System. Data from: Researchers Data Collation

regulations, it can be seen that the Chinese government's supervision of the traditional auto insurance market tends to be mature and comprehensive (see Fig. 4).

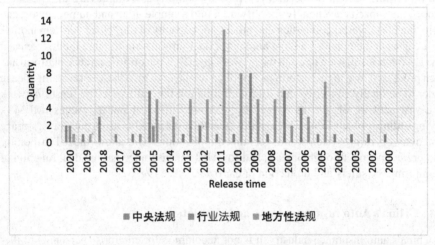

Fig. 4. Number of existing auto insurance regulations in China. Data from: Researchers Data Collation

For Different from it, UBI entered China's auto insurance market in 2014 and became a new type of insurance in China. Up to now, UBI has only been mentioned once in the auto insurance management documents of the Chinese government. Article 3 of the *Guiding Opinions on Implementing Comprehensive Reform of Auto Insurance* issued by China Banking and Insurance Regulatory Commission in 2020: "3. Expand and Optimize Commercial Auto Insurance Guarantee Services (IX) Enriching Commercial Auto Insurance Products" mentions UBI as an innovative product. But at present, the special regulations for UBI have not yet appeared, from which we can see that the government's supervision of UBI still has a big improvement stage.

4 CHINA's Regulatory Measures for IoT UBI

4.1 Legislative Supervision

Because of the insufficient supervision of laws and regulations, the Chinese government can adjust and revise the relevant contents based on the original traditional auto insurance, improve the provisions and specifications of IoT UBI in the law, and build targeted provisions and specifications of IoT UBI characterized by big data and intelligence of IoT UBI. On the other hand, according to the characteristics of IoT UBI relying on big data, the legislation allows on-board diagnosis system and driving place in the data system besides video, video and audio as evidence of case trial. Set up industry-specific laws and regulations specifically for the network leakage of personal privacy information. Take IoT UBI privacy as an experiment to carry out preliminary effective management of privacy.

4.2 Supervision from Government

The government gives IoT UBI research assistance when necessary, but prohibits administrators from threatening money. Otherwise, it will eventually lead to the cessation of research, the company will face the consequences of bankruptcy, and the relevant personnel will be criminally punished for the crime of corruption. Administrative organs should relax the supervision of IoT UBI properly and not interfere with the development of IoT UBI in the auto insurance market too much. The government can give appropriate long-term preferential policies to technology companies that study IoT UBI, insurance companies that carry out IoT UBI business, network car platforms that purchase IoT UBI and individual car owners to stimulate the vitality of IoT UBI in the Chinese market.

Finally, since the fields and industries involved in IoT UBI are too complicated, the regulatory framework is unclear, and the system is difficult to establish, governments at all levels should standardize the specific regulatory authorities of IoT UBI in various regions, that is, clearly stipulate who supervises and how to supervise IoT UBI in many fields of the market.

4.3 Supervision of Enterprises

Enterprises should reasonably regulate the use of car owners' information rights, that is, they can access information data that does not touch the privacy of private car owners; For private information data involving car owners, it is necessary to seek the wishes of car owners, otherwise, relevant information data cannot be illegally accessed. If the circumstances are serious after illegal use, it can be cited in the field of criminal law. Companies that steal more than 5,000 people's data within one to five years should be criminally punished for the crime of occupational embezzlement; If there are no more than 5,000 people, the company shall be criminally punished for the crime of infringing personal information. The research of data technology takes a long time and the results are different. The success of research needs more data information, so it is measured according to the number of illegal access; Third, it is stipulated that employees of enterprises shall not provide all the information of users to others or other units outside the public platform of the company without obtaining instructions from the company, and shall not illegally sell or provide private information of users to others or units. If employees violate the former, they will be punished according to the relevant articles of association; Violating the latter will be punished according to the crime of infringing personal information.

5 Conclusion

IoT UBI shows greater functional advantages and development prospects under the combination of technology companies and insurance institutions. Under such a new product with diversified functions, it can't achieve good development without the supervision and control of the government. The analysis of the combination of electronic information technology companies and insurance companies China IoT IoT UBI Car Insurance System and the existing auto insurance regulatory documents of the Chinese government shows that IoT UBI is in a good development trend in China; but, the supervision of IoT UBI by the Chinese government is still lagging, that is, the supervision policy is lacking, the supervision structure is unclear, and the system is difficult to establish. Due to the small length of the article and the limited data collected, it can not fully reflect the whole development system of IoT UBI in China and other subtle problems. However, the analysis of some representative insurance institutions and technology companies shows the general status quo and existing problems of IoT UBI development in China, that is, the mature development of IoT UBI in China in the future needs the strengthening of Chinese government supervision, the refinement of auto insurance laws and regulations, and the concretization of administrative supervision departments for the development of IoT UBI in China.

Acknowledgements. This work was supported by Foundation for Advanced Talents of Yulin Normal University (G2019SK02)

References

Dai Jianguo, F.: Research on reducing asymmetric information of auto insurance based on UBI. J. Changzhou Ins. Technol. **28**, 44–49 (2015)

Han Changyin, F.: Reconstruction of driving behavior insurance and auto insurance norms. Journal of Shanghai Jiaotong University **28**, 32–46 (2020)

Jiang Yu, F.: Dilemma and Countermeasures of UBI. Shanghai Insurance Monthly **3**, 31–37 (2020)

Li Siyao, F.: Development trend and challenge of driving behavior research under intelligent networking environment-actuarial science based on driving risk. J. Highw. Transp. Res. Develop. **32**, 37–43 (2017)

Liu Jian, F.: Research and practice of ubi based on commercial vehicle networking. J. Chengdu Electromecha. College **22**, 48–53 (2019)

Ren Yuan, F.: Research on the Application of Insurance Technology in Accurate Premium Determination. Pass College of Chongqing Technology and Business University, pp. 324–327 (2019)

Shao Chengyin, F.: Learn from American experience to Develop UBI with Chinese Characteristics. Shanghai Insurance Monthly **8**, 48–53 (2018)

Sun Hongtao, F.: Research on the Construction of UBI System in China. Journal of Law Application **3**, 25–32 (2020)

Wang Li, F.: UBI design based on vehicle cycle behavior. Measurement & Control Technology **36**(12), 142–145 (2017)

Wu Xiangyou, F.: UBI pricing model based on driving behavior. J. Univ. Electr. Sci. Technol. China **22**(4), 67–76 (2020)

Zhang Haixia, F.: Research on key technologies of intelligent vehicle networking based on vehicle behavior analysis. J. Electr. Info. Technol. **42**, 36–49 (2020)

Zhu Jiazhen, F.: Research on data notification and protection mechanism of UBI under IOV. Financial Regulation Research **8**, 102–114 (2020)

Constructing a Violence Recognition Technique for Elderly Patients with Lower Limb Disability

Lun-Ping Hung[1]([✉]), Chih-Wei Yang[1], Li-Hui Lee[2], and Chien-Liang Chen[3]

[1] Department of Information Management, National Taipei University of Nursing and Health Sciences, Taipei, Taiwan, R.O.C.
lunping@ntunhs.edu.tw
[2] Department of Health Care Management, National Taipei University of Nursing and Health Sciences, Taipei, Taiwan, R.O.C.
[3] Department of Innovative Living Design, Overseas Chinese University, Taichung, Taiwan, R.O.C.

Abstract. Elder abuse has been recognized as an important public health problem, and will become increasingly serious as the world's population ages. Therefore, the first problem that needs to be solved is the detection of the incident by the outside world. This study proposes a real-time abuse detection method based on OpenPose, an open source human posture tracking technology. By extracting the posture information of people in the care field, we can further analyze the posture status and mutual position, as well as the changes of current and previous movements, and determine whether there are abuse events in the field. This design allows the family to be notified in case of suspected abuse to protect the rights of the elderly from being violated.

Keywords: Elder abuse · Violence detection · OpenPose · Home care

1 Introduction

Violence can bring people a lot of harm both in psychological or physical aspects. Special attention needs to be paid to the violence toward the elderly, as the violence toward the elderly has been recognized as an important public health issue. According to the definition of the World Health Organization (WHO), elder abuse refers to a single or repeated act or lack of appropriate action occurring within any relationship where there is an expectation of trust, which causes harm or distress to an older person [1]. The results of past research have pointed out that nearly one-sixth of the elderly have been subjected to violence within a year. The number of elderly people in the world was as high as 141 million at the time of the study, and if the same ratio is maintained, the number of elderly people subject to violence is estimated to be 330 million by 2050 [2]. Violence will cause great physical and psychological harm to the victims, and may further affect their health. Therefore, how to protect the rights of the elderly and avoid incidents are issues that need to be paid attention to. However, the occurrence of violent

© ICST Institute for Computer Sciences, Social Informatics and Telecommunications Engineering 2022
Published by Springer Nature Switzerland AG 2022. All Rights Reserved
Y.-B. Lin et al. (Eds.): SGIoT 2021, LNICST 447, pp. 24–37, 2022.
https://doi.org/10.1007/978-3-031-20398-5_3

behavior is usually during the caregiver's care process, when there are only two people, the caregiver and the care recipient in most cases, and the incident needs to be notified by the care recipient or a third party (e.g., family members). But in the past, the persons being cared for were all disadvantaged parties, and even if they had the opportunity to report, they might not dare to speak out due to their own physical or psychological barriers, communication skills, fear of being taken into custody or receiving retaliation [3]. This has led to the fact that such violence can only be discovered by family members or a third-party non-primary caregiver a long time after its occurrence, and may even be revealed after the death of the elderly.

Violent behaviors do not take place suddenly. It is mostly caused by a long-term accumulation which consumes the patience of the caregiver, leading to physical and psychological fatigue of the caregiver and resulting in violent behaviors. In addition, if the care recipient has mental problems, the situation will become more serious. Mental health problems have been proved to be indirectly related to violent behaviors [4]. Elderly people with mental problems especially need the assistance of caregivers, which will also increase the risk. However, according to a report by Alzheimer's Disease International (ADI) in 2019, it is estimated that there are more than 50 million people with dementia in the world, and the number is expected to grow to 152 million by 2050, equivalent to one more person suffering from dementia every 3 s from now on [5]. And, the results of past studies have shown that dementia is closely related to age, which means that the probability of this disease will be higher as people are getting older [6].

However, as per the data released by Ministry of Health and Welfare of Taiwan in 2018, Taiwan has officially entered the aged society as the proportion of the elderly over 65 years old accounted for 14.56% of the total population, and it is estimated that this proportion will be as high as 20% by 2025. This figure means that Taiwan will enter the stage of a super-aged society soon [7]. While the proportion of the elderly population is so high, the number of people with dementia in Taiwan is estimated to have exceeded 290,000 by the end of 2019, and by 2061 the cumulative number will be as high as 880,000, which is equivalent to 5 out of every 100 people in Taiwan suffering from dementia [8]. The above trends are already irreversible problems, and while trying to slow down or even improve the situation, what we need to resolve is how to protect the rights and interests of the elderly with dementia from being violated.

Under normal circumstances, it was possible to improve and solve through external assistance when dealing with unreasonable treatment or even infringing on one's rights and interests, but if the above factors of communication skills, being afraid of retaliation or suffering from mental diseases are considered, the discovery of the occurrence of the incident may be more difficult. In the past, some family members installed cameras in the home care field to record the overall care process, and add more protection to the elders in the care process via achieving the remote real-time monitoring effect through the Internet. But the family members cannot check the condition of the home every minute and every second, which makes it impossible to know the situation immediately when the incident occurs. Therefore, it is still impossible to effectively safeguard the elders' safety.

In summary, the main purpose of this study is to ensure that the elders are not treated violently while being cared for. By using cameras installed in the care field, the situation in the field is captured and the images are automatically identified for real-time detection of whether there is a violent incident, and real-time notification of the family members of the elders at the moment of the incident to protect the rights of the elders from being infringed. The overall structure of this study is introduced in 6 chapters. Section 2 reviews the research related to human activity recognition, Sect. 3 describes the data set acquisition and image human posture extraction, Sect. 4 introduces the violent behavior detection method proposed by this study, Sect. 5 presents the analysis of results after the experiments, and Sect. 6 describes the overall research results of this paper.

2 Literature Review

Violence can bring people a lot of harm both in psychological or physical aspects. Special attention needs to be paid to the violence toward the elderly, as the violence toward the elderly has been recognized as an important public health issue. According to the definition of the World Health Organization (WHO), elder abuse refers to a single or repeated act or lack of appropriate action occurring within any relationship where there is an expectation of trust, which causes harm or distress to an older person [1]. The results of past research have pointed out that nearly one-sixth of the elderly have been subjected to violence within a year. The number of elderly people in the world was as high as 141 million at the time of the study, and if the same ratio is maintained, the number of elderly people subject to violence is estimated to be 330 million by 2050 [2]. Violence will cause great physical and psychological harm to the victims, and may further affect their health. Therefore, how to protect the rights of the elderly and avoid incidents are issues that need to be paid attention to. However, the occurrence of violent behavior is usually during the caregiver's care process, when there are only two people, the caregiver and the care recipient in most cases, and the incident needs to be notified by the care recipient or a third party (e.g., family members). But in the past, the persons being cared for were all disadvantaged parties, and even if they had the opportunity to report, they might not dare to speak out due to their own physical or psychological barriers, communication skills, fear of being taken into custody or receiving retaliation [3]. This has led to the fact that such violence can only be discovered by family members or a third-party non-primary caregiver a long time after its occurrence, and may even be revealed after the death of the elderly.

Violent behaviors do not take place suddenly. It is mostly caused by a long-term accumulation which consumes the patience of the caregiver, leading to physical and psychological fatigue of the caregiver and resulting in violent behaviors. In addition, if the care recipient has mental problems, the situation will become more serious. Mental health problems have been proved to be indirectly related to violent behaviors [4]. Elderly people with mental problems especially need the assistance of caregivers, which will also increase the risk. However, according to a report by Alzheimer's Disease International (ADI) in 2019, it is estimated that there are more than 50 million people with dementia in the world, and the number is expected to grow to 152 million by 2050, equivalent to one more person suffering from dementia every 3 s from now on [5]. And, the results of past studies have shown that dementia is closely related to age, which means that the probability of this disease will be higher as people are getting older [6].

However, as per the data released by Ministry of Health and Welfare of Taiwan in 2018, Taiwan has officially entered the aged society as the proportion of the elderly over 65 years old accounted for 14.56% of the total population, and it is estimated that this proportion will be as high as 20% by 2025. This figure means that Taiwan will enter the stage of a super-aged society soon [7]. While the proportion of the elderly population is so high, the number of people with dementia in Taiwan is estimated to have exceeded 290,000 by the end of 2019, and by 2061 the cumulative number will be as high as 880,000, which is equivalent to 5 out of every 100 people in Taiwan suffering from dementia [8]. The above trends are already irreversible problems, and while trying to slow down or even improve the situation, what we need to resolve is how to protect the rights and interests of the elderly with dementia from being violated.

Under normal circumstances, it was possible to improve and solve through external assistance when dealing with unreasonable treatment or even infringing on one's rights and interests, but if the above factors of communication skills, being afraid of retaliation or suffering from mental diseases are considered, the discovery of the occurrence of the incident may be more difficult. In the past, some family members installed cameras in the home care field to record the overall care process, and add more protection to the elders in the care process via achieving the remote real-time monitoring effect through the Internet. But the family members cannot check the condition of the home every minute and every second, which makes it impossible to know the situation immediately when the incident occurs. Therefore, it is still impossible to effectively safeguard the elders' safety.

In summary, the main purpose of this study is to ensure that the elders are not treated violently while being cared for. By using cameras installed in the care field, the situation in the field is captured and the images are automatically identified for real-time detection of whether there is a violent incident, and real-time notification of the family members of the elders at the moment of the incident to protect the rights of the elders from being infringed. The overall structure of this study is introduced in 6 chapters. Section 2 reviews the research related to human activity recognition, Sect. 3 describes the data set acquisition and image human posture extraction, Sect. 4 introduces the violent behavior detection method proposed by this study, Sect. 5 presents the analysis of results after the experiments, and Sect. 6 describes the overall research results of this paper.

2.1 Posture Detection Method Based on Human Skeleton Extraction

Since the composition of the human body posture is based on the relative positions of the bones, most of the human body posture recognition using pictures and images takes the bones as the basis for judgment. The common evaluation methods can be divided into depth images and RGB images. For the former one, the depth images, the joint position information is evaluated and converted by using the information received by a sensor of special distance and depth to infer the posture of the human body. For the latter, the RGM images, the principle of determination is mainly to piece together the skeleton of the human body with key nodes through the detection of the key bone nodes of the human body in the image [9].

Human Posture Detection Application Based on Depth Image
Kinect is a device for deep image recognition launched by Microsoft in 2010. This device can automatically recognize 20 joint points of the human body without the human body wearing any equipment and then infer the skeleton of the human body [10]. The obtained information can also be used for extended applications in various fields. For example, Bereket et al. used Kinect to calculate the energy consumption of the human body in physical training activities. They recorded the exercise with this device, and analyzed and compared the obtained information with the acceleration sensor worn on the body. The final result showed that using this mode can effectively replace the detection method of the traditional acceleration sensor, and achieve higher precision applications [11]. Kinect was used by Shrivastava et al. in human gait detection. By photographing the angle and distance between the feet and the ground when the human body is walking, it can determine whether there is an abnormal condition, so as to further infer the health of the subject [12].

Human Posture Detection Application Based on RGB Image
OpenPose is a human posture detection method developed on the basis of deep learning. It was released by the research team of Carnegie Mellon University (CMU) in 2017 and can be used in the multi-person real-time detection of 2D images and video images. The area where the human shape is in the image and the video can be automatically detected with this method and a total of 135 feature points for the humanoid body, face, hands, and feet can be marked. Different from the aforementioned depths image of Kinect, the image input by OpenPose is an ordinary RGB image, which does not contain the distance information of the depth image. Therefore, recognition can be carried out with the image obtained by the ordinary camera alone [13]. In related applications, Hang et al. created a home rehabilitation system using OpenPose, Kalman filter, and Full Convolutional Neural Network (FCN) to improve the rehabilitation effect of patients at home to resolve the problem of poor results due to the lack of physicians' nursing guidance in the process of stroke patients' rehabilitation at home, and the results showed very high adaptability to the interference of the background environment [14].

2.2 Analysis and Comparison Based on the Human Skeleton Extraction Method

As mentioned above, many human posture applications based on skeleton extraction have good results and feasibility, whether using depth images or RGB images, but there are still some differences in recognition between the two detection methods. Therefore, the accuracy and effectiveness of both methods are discussed in this paragraph. Woojoo et al. used Kinect and OpenPose respectively to assess the risk of musculoskeletal diseases, and mainly compared the difference between the two methods in occlusion and non-human front conditions. The content of the evaluation was the measured joint angle and RULA/REBA ergonomic posture scores, and the final research results showed that there was not much difference between the two methods without occlusion. But, in the occlusion and non-frontal situations, there was a significant decrease in the accuracy of

Kinect, leading to a large error, while OpenPose was still more accurate although there was a certain degree of influence [15]. In addition, Megumi et al. also used OpenPose and the VICON 3D motion analysis system simultaneously to perform a comparative analysis of the bilateral squat posture to explore the reliability of human posture detection methods. The verification results indicated that the joint angle detection data of the two were almost identical, which is sufficient to prove that this method can be effectively used in the field of motion analysis [16].

2.3 Violent Incident Detection Based on Image Recognition

Contact between people is inevitable in the real world, but, in the process of inter-action, there may be conflicts between the two parties due to different ideas or other factors. Taking public places as an example, several security staffs or guards are usually assigned to mediate this type of problems, but there is a certain gap between manpower and the associated field space in fact, and human observation alone cannot effectively pay attention to the real-time conditions of each area in the field. The intervention of information technology can effectively alleviate this problem. For example, Dinesh et al. used Histogram of Oriented Gradients (HOG) to extract feature values from images in order to solve conflicts and violence in football fields, and labeled them as the three nonviolent models of the human body, violence, and non-violence. Then, the data were all imported into the Bidirectional Long Short-Term Memory (BDLSTM) network for overall training. Finally, it was verified that the system's real-time detection accuracy for violent incidents was as high as 94.5% with robustness [17]. Saif et al. proposed that the previous violence detection methods often failed to present robust detection results due to noise, lack of appropriate feature selection, and effective classification methods. Therefore, they used compressed images to merge the same colors in the background to minimize the complexity of the background and proposed the combination of the angle and linear distance of the light with a Kalman filter to achieve the effect of noise reduc-tion, and a Random Forest (RF) was used at the end as a classifier to achieve the 99.12% accuracy at a frame rate of 35 FPS [18]. Pujol et al. proposed a smart city application concept, using cameras set up in the city to automatically detect violent incidents. The characteristic parameters such as the degree of eccentricity and acceleration of light were extracted through the Fourier transform, Histogram of Optical Acceleration (HOA), and Histogram of Spatial Gradient of Acceleration (HSGA) aiming at the acceleration dif-ference between every two frames of the acquired image, and a support vector machine was adopted as a classifier. The final accuracy was between 85 and 97%, and it was effective [19].

This paragraph discusses two mainstream human skeleton extraction methods, both of which are image detection methods that can achieve the detection of human posture characteristics without requiring the participants to wear any sensors. In terms of the difference between the two methods, the depth image needs to be equipped with a special distance sensor such as Kinect, while in general, the surveillance equipment in the care field is not equipped with this special sensor. At the same time, it was pointed out in the past studies that the accuracy of recognition by OpenPose has higher performance both in the situation where there is an objection occlusion or the human body is not frontal and the detection accuracy. Therefore, the detection method of OpenPose is more suitable for the situation in this study.

3   Data Collection and Human Skeleton Extraction

3.1   Data Collection in Daily Care Environment

The main purpose of this study was to ensure that the care recipients can avoid the risk of violent treatment during the process of receiving care. The targeted groups include the elders with difficulties in seeking help from the outside world, physical and mental disabilities, or mental illnesses such as dementia. It is difficult to obtain a large amount of image data. Therefore, we asked several volunteers to perform role-playing in different situations in this study. However, there may be many pieces of furniture or other objects in the field. Although the results of past research showed that OpenPose has a fairly stable detection ability in the face of a complex background and object occlusion, the camera angle and distance were adjusted to achieve a better shooting position to avoid unnecessary errors and improve the detection effect. The obtained images are shown in Fig. 1. The situation may include the following 3 conditions:

(1)   The situation in which only one care recipient is included in the field. Since it requires more than two people to achieve a violent behavior, this situation is a general care situation.
(2)   The situation where there are two or more people including the caregiver and the care recipient in the field, and this is a normal care behavior. For example, in this situation, the caregiver on the left is handing a water cup to the care recipient. Although there is an action of contact, it is a reminder action rather than a harmful action.
(3)   The situation in which there are two persons, the caregiver, and the care recipient, and violent behavior occurs in the field. For example, in this situation, the caregiver on the left is waving his arm quickly to the care recipient. Since the movement is quick and drastic, there may be a violent behavior.

This study collected a total of 1500 incident conditions, including three types of simulation of general care situations (single person), general care situations (multiple persons), and violent behavior situations. Each of the three types has 100, 500, and 900 incidents, respectively. The time of each situation was 3 to 6 s, and each second contains 13 to 15 frames. The obtained incident images were used in the subsequent model training and judgment actions.

3.2   Human Skeleton Extraction Based on OpenPose

To judge human behaviors through images, the first action is to determine the position of the human body and its posture in the acquired image. Using OpenPose human skeleton recognition technology can automatically detect the human-shaped area in the image and mark it, such as shown in Fig. 2. In the absence of any object occlusion, the detected

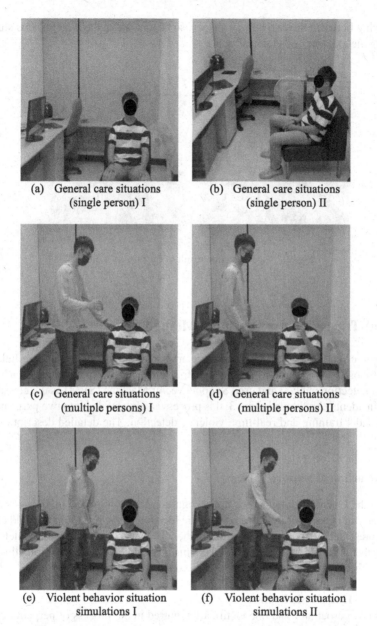

(a) General care situations
(single person) I

(b) General care situations
(single person) II

(c) General care situations
(multiple persons) I

(d) General care situations
(multiple persons) II

(e) Violent behavior situation
simulations I

(f) Violent behavior situation
simulations II

Fig. 1. Simulation of general care and violent behavior situations

humanoid image will mark 18 key nodes, and a straight line will be marked between the corresponding two points to estimate the positions of the skeleton and bones of the human body. In this way, the image captured by the camera is pre-processed, and then the posture presented by the human skeleton can be classified with the corresponding relationship between the two human shapes, so as to achieve the target of this study of detecting the existence of violence or not.

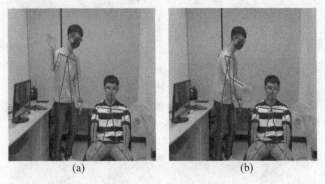

(a)   (b)

Fig. 2. Node detection result of the human skeleton

4   Real-Time Violence Detection Method

In order to effectively detect whether there are violent incidents in the care field, this study proposed the operation process and four characteristic parameters of a violent behavior detection method and used Support Vector Machine (SVM) as the classifier of violent incidents. As shown in Fig. 3, this process can be divided into two parts, namely offline model training and real-time violence detection. The detailed description is as follows:

4.1   Extraction of Feature Values

Through the OpenPose human posture recognition technology, the human skeleton in the image can be effectively detected, and the location of the person in the field and the posture presented can be obtained by this method. However, it is not possible to determine whether there is a violent incident based on this information alone. Therefore, this study proposed the following four features as subsequent judgment parameters.

Number of Human Skeletons

At least one perpetrator and one victim are required in the process of perpetrating violence. Therefore, the number of people in the field will be the most important key. For example, there is only the care recipient in the field, and the key element will not be established in a violent behavior.

Distance Between Human Skeletons

This parameter is the distance between the caregiver and the care recipient. The distance between the two will have a certain degree of impact on the occurrence of violent incidents. For example, if the distance between the two is too far and they cannot touch

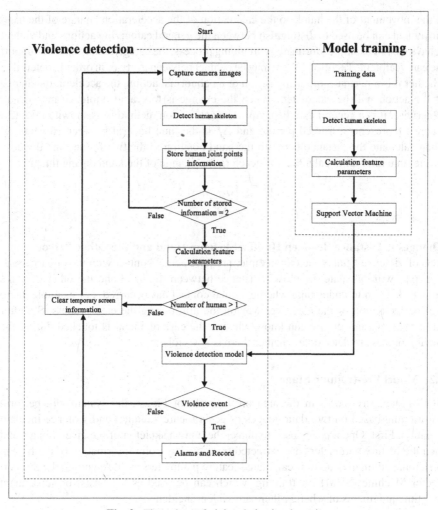

Fig. 3. Flow chart of violent behavior detection

each other, it will not be easy to have the possibility of violent incidents. The calculation method is to use the Euclidean formula, as shown in Eq. (1), where x_i means the center coordinates of the human skeleton, and y_i represents the center coordinates of another human skeleton, and this formula is used to calculate the distance between the two.

$$\left(\sum_{i=1}^{n} |x_i - y_i|^2 \right)^{1/2} \tag{1}$$

Changes in Human Skeleton Hand Acceleration
In the care process, the caregiver needs to engage in many care actions, and sometimes he or she may even need to touch the patient's body, and most of the actions belong

to the movement of the hand, so the calculation of the acceleration change of the hand movement can be used to distinguish between the general caregiving actions and violent behaviors. For example, during the caregiving process, the caregiver may need to support the care recipient. Therefore, there may be contact between the two. In order to determine whether it is a normal supporting action or an abnormal action, the acceleration change of the action will be calculated. When the change is too rapid, violence may occur. Otherwise, it is a general care behavior. The calculation method is as shown in Eq. (2), where f represents a framed picture and Δf is the time interval between two frames. Then calculate the distance between the hand position in the two frames and divide it by the time interval to calculate the acceleration change of the hand during this time.

$$\frac{\left(\sum_{i=1}^{n} |x_i - y_i|^2\right)^{1/2}}{\Delta f} \tag{2}$$

Changes in Distance Between Human Skeleton Hand and the Other Person
Acts of violence against the care recipient require actual contact with the other person. This part will calculate the closest distance between the hand and the other person's human skeleton to understand whether actual contact has occurred. For example, there will be the action of the caregiver waving the arm during the care process. So, after adding this parameter, we can know whether the care recipient is touched during the waving process to determine whether there is any violence.

4.2 Model Pre-training Stage

At this stage, as shown in the area on the right of Fig. 3, the system will perform pre-training based on two data images of general care situation and violence incident situation. First, OpenPose is used to detect the human skeleton of the given image, and then the feature parameters are extracted from the key point information of the human skeleton, and finally, the four calculated feature parameters are thrown into the Support Vector Machine (SVM) for training, which can be used as the basis for subsequent real-time judgments of whether there are violent incidents.

4.3 Real-Time Violence Detection Stage

At this stage, as shown in the left area of Fig. 3, real-time detection can be carried out after the model is built. First, the system will capture the image captured by the camera in real-time, and then perform the detection through the OpenPose screen. When the presence of a person in the field is successfully detected, the human skeleton and position of the person can be obtained, and then the screen information can be stored. If the number of stored information fails to reach two groups, the comparison and calculation of features cannot be performed. Therefore, the above actions need to be performed again, and the four characteristic parameters described in Sect. 4.1 are calculated after the conditions are met. However, the establishment of a violent incident requires two or more people, so if the number of people detected is less than two, no follow-up actions will be taken and all the temporary screen information will be cleared. Otherwise, the four characteristic parameters are given to the built model to determine whether there is a violent incident.

5   Results

In order to prove that the real-time detection effect can be effectively carried out when violent behavior occurs, this section will further verify the detection method. First, as explained above, the presence of only one person will not constitute an element of a violent incident. Therefore, this situation is classified as a general care situation, and the rest are also violent incident situations, and then all the collected image data were divided into a training set and a test set at a ratio of 8:2, as shown in Table 1. After the four characteristic parameters of the number of human skeletons, the distance between the human skeletons, the acceleration change of the human skeleton's hand and the change in the distance between the human skeleton's hand and the other person were calculated from the data set, and then the SVM was used for classification to determine whether there are any incidents of violent behavior. ⁻

Table 1. Distribution of number of images for the general care and violent behaviors

Type	Total	Training (80%)	Test (20%)
General care behavior	600	480	120
Violent behavior	900	720	180

In the overall detection process of this study, violent behavior was defined as a positive sample, and general care behavior was defined as a negative sample. Therefore, after classification, there were four situations. (TP): the actual occurrence of a violent behavior, and it is predicted as a violent behavior; (TN): the actual general care behavior, and it is predicted as a general care behavior; (FN): the actual occurrence of a violent behavior, but the predicted result is a general care behavior; (FP): the actual general care behavior, but the prediction result is a violent behavior. The four values of Accuracy, Precision, Specificity, and Recall of the model were calculated to verify the model.

Table 2. Confusion matrix of support vector machine

Type	Violent behavior	General care behavior
Violent behavior	746	91
General care behavior	154	509

The results obtained after five-fold cross-validation are shown in Table 2. Accuracy was 83.67%, Precision was 89.13%, Specificity was 84.83% and Recall was 82.89%. The results showed that in most cases, this violent behavior detection method could effectively detect when violent behaviors occur, and had a very high distinguishing ability in determining general care behaviors. However, in the case of the perpetrator's small motion range or slow swing speed, identification errors may occur. In addition, since the research fields were all indoors, there were occlusions by other objects such as furniture. As a result, humanoid node detection cannot be accurately extracted, so that subsequent judgment errors occurred.

6 Conclusions

Violence may occur in people's surroundings without being noticed. The occurrence of violence can bring irreparable physical and psychological damage to the victim. For the elderly, the damage caused by violence will be even greater. In recent years, violence to the elderly has been defined as an important issue that needs attention, and due to the increasingly serious problem of aging of the world's population, more and more elderly people need to be taken care of. With the increase of age, the elderly are more likely to suffer from mental disorders such as dementia than the average person. As a result, even if they are subjected to violent treatment, they cannot effectively seek help from the outside world. Therefore, this study proposed a violent behavior detection method to automatically detect violent behavior in the care field. First, the OpenPose human body posture recognition technology was adopted by the method to detect the image taken by the camera and extract the posture and position of the person in the field, four characteristic parameters from the obtained human skeleton information were calculated, and the Support Vector Machine (SVM) was used as the classifier to identify whether there is a violent incident in the field domain. The final result showed that the accuracy was as high as 83.67%. Although there may be identification errors for body movements with small movements or slow speeds, however, in most cases, this method can effectively detect violent incidents. This method can help the elderly not to have their rights infringed during the care process, and can effectively detect when violent incidents occur to reduce and improve the problem of elder abuse, which is of great significance.

This study achieved a good effect on the detection of violent behavior of caregivers in the home care field, but there is still some room for improvement:

(1) The current problem that small or slow detailed movements cannot be effectively detected should be addressed, so as to improve the accuracy and precision of recognition and reduce the occurrence of judgment errors.
(2) The image data collected in this study were all located in the controllable experimental field. In the future, the practical application in the home care field can be tried, and more complex scenes and furnishings can be added to verify the usability and effectiveness of this method.
(3) When an incident is determined as a suspected violent behavior, the family member of the care recipient should be immediately informed, so that the family member can understand the condition of the care recipient for the first time, and provide corresponding assistance.

References

1. Organization: W.H., Elder abuse (2021)

2. Yon, Y., et al.: Elder abuse prevalence in community settings: a systematic review and meta-analysis. Lancet Glob Health **5**(2), e147–e156 (2017)
3. Baker, P.R.A., et al.: Interventions for preventing abuse in the elderly. The Cochrane database of systematic reviews **2016**(8), CD010321-CD010321 (2016)
4. Storey, J.E.: Risk factors for elder abuse and neglect: A review of the literature. Aggression and Violent Behavior **50**, 101339 (2020)
5. International: A.s.D., Attitudes to dementia (2019)
6. Sun, Y., et al.: A nationwide survey of mild cognitive impairment and dementia, including very mild dementia, in taiwan. PLOS ONE **9**(6), e100303 (2014)
7. Council: N.D., Taiwan Population Projection (2020)
8. Welfare, M.O.H.A.: Policy Framework and Action Plan for Dementia Prevention and Care 2.0 (2021)
9. Chen, W., et al.: Fall Detection Based on Key Points of Human-Skeleton Using OpenPose. Symmetry **12**(5) (2020)
10. Yeung, L.-F., et al.: Effects of camera viewing angles on tracking kinematic gait patterns using Azure Kinect, Kinect v2 and Orbbec Astra Pro v2. Gait & Posture **87**, 19–26 (2021)
11. Woldegiorgis, B.H., Lin, C.J., Sananta, R.: Using Kinect body joint detection system to predict energy expenditures during physical activities. Applied Ergonomics **97**, 103540 (2021)
12. Shrivastava, S., Bharti, J., Pateriya, R.K.: Machine learning based gait abnormality detection using Microsoft Kinect sensor. Materials Today: Proceedings (2021)
13. Cao, Z., et al.: OpenPose: realtime multi-person 2D pose estimation using part affinity fields. IEEE Transactions on Pattern Analysis and Machine Intelligence **43**(1), 172–186 (2021)
14. Yan, H., et al.: Real-Time Continuous Human Rehabilitation Action Recognition using Open-Pose and FCN. In: 2020 3rd International Conference on Advanced Electronic Materials, Computers and Software Engineering (AEMCSE) (2020)
15. Kim, W., et al.: Ergonomic postural assessment using a new open-source human pose estimation technology (OpenPose). Int. J. Indus. Ergonom. **84**, 103164 (2021)
16. Ota, M., et al.: Verification of reliability and validity of motion analysis systems during bilateral squat using human pose tracking algorithm. Gait & Posture **80**, 62–67 (2020)
17. Samuel R.D.J., et al.: Real time violence detection framework for football stadium comprising of big data analysis and deep learning through bidirectional LSTM. Computer Networks **151**, 191–200 (2019)
18. Saif, A.F.M., Mahayuddin, Z.: Moment Features based Violence Action Detection using Optical Flow. Int. J. Adva. Comp. Sci. Appli. **11** (2020)
19. Pujol, F.A., Mora, H., Pertegal, M.L.: A soft computing approach to violence detection in social media for smart cities. Soft Computing **24**(15), 11007–11017 (2020)

Aquaculture Monitoring Systems Based on Lightweight Kubernetes and Rancher

Halim Fathoni[1,2], Chao-Tung Yang[3,4]([⊠]), Chin-Yin Huang[1],
Chien-Yi Chen[3], and Tí-Fēng Hsieh[3]

[1] Department Industrial Engineering and Enterprise Information,
Tunghai University, Taichung, Taiwan (R.O.C.)
{D07330701,huangcy}@thu.edu.tw
[2] Department Ekonomi dan Bisnis, Politeknik Negeri Lampung, Bandar Lampung,
Indonesia
fathoni@polinela.ac.id
[3] Department Computer Science, Tunghai University, Taichung, Taiwan (R.O.C.)
[4] Research Center for Smart Sustainable Circular Economy, Tunghai University,
No. 1727, Sec. 4, Taiwan Boulevard, Taichung 407224, Taiwan (R.O.C.)
ctyang@thu.edu.tw

Abstract. Edge Computing is the new paradigm to process data at the edge of the network. The scenario of edge computing varies, depending on the case and problem. In this paper, we investigate an architecture that is suitable for Intelligence Aquaculture. This system will handle tasks such as collecting the water sensor data and running an Artificial Intelligence algorithm to train model prediction and run real-time object detection with a Deep learning algorithm and Deepstream. All applications were deployed with a docker container and managed with Lightweight Kubernetes (K3s). Rancher is also used to coordinate and visualize the resource system of the edge devices. This system architecture could be a reference for edge computing ecosystems and monitoring system of Aquaculture.

Keywords: Edge computing · Edge AI · Lightweight Kubernetes · K3s · Rancher · Aquaculture

1 Introduction

Nowadays, the use of the internet of things creates new challenges for cloud computing. In the cloud computing paradigm, data is stored centrally in the data center. However, sometimes real-time response and low latency become a burden for Cloud Computing when dealing with emerging technologies such as smart cities or Smart Aquaculture. Some researchers propose a new computing paradigm as extended of Cloud computing as known as Edge Computing. Edge computing is a paradigm where the resources of an edge server are placed at the edge of the network close to the things or data sources, integrating the capabilities of networks, storage, and applications [3]. Generally, the edge of the

Y.-B. Lin et al. (Eds.): SGIoT 2021, LNICST 447, pp. 38–45, 2022.
https://doi.org/10.1007/978-3-031-20398-5_4

networks is located only one hop away from the associated end devices. The purpose is to reduce network transmission, reduce response time and increase the security for data privacy. Some intelligence services also deploy to meet the key requirements of industry digitization for agile connectivity, real-time data optimization, and application intelligence [2]. Recently, Intelligence applications cannot be avoided by edge computing. Machine Learning and Deep Learning are commonly used in Traditional Cloud Computing. Data send to the cloud, and then the best model will support inference in the edge devices to deploy services.

The development of Edge Computing is still growing. Some researcher has proposed some edge computing architecture, for example, Cloudlet [5], Fog Computing [15], Microdata Center [8], Multi-Access Edge computing [7] and other systems [11] that work on the edge of the network which has same principles but different focuses. However, there has not yet been consensus on standardized definitions, architectures, and protocols of edge computing.

This work investigates an architecture that is suitable for Intelligence Aquaculture architecture. Aquaculture is one of the ways to ensure good seafood for the world [14]. Nowadays, traditional aquaculture faces severe environmental pollution, diseases, and a lack of product traceability [4]. Through Edge Computing principles, it is needed a fundamental architecture that can use for Intelligence Aquaculture. This Architecture will use a container to ensure an efficient deployment in every edge device, and all containers will be orchestrated with lightweight Kubernetes K3s.

This article is structured as follows: Sect. 2 Literature Review of the technologies in the architecture; Sect. 3 presents the design architecture; Sect. 4 presents the performance result of our architecture; Sect. 5 is discussion.

2   Literature Review

2.1   LoraWAN

LoraWAN is an open standard for link and network layers that operate on top of LoRa as the physical layers [12]. LoraWAN is one of LPWAN technologies where it uses low power and long-range communication. This technology is suitable for rural areas with an insufficient infrastructure of Wi-Fi or a similar network for sending data to a server. LoraWAN can cover around 20km in the line-of-sight situation, and it was designed to work on unlicensed frequency bands (433MHz, 868MHz, or 915Mhz) depend on a regulator of the area. LoraWan focuses on uplinks for efficient power usage. The use of two-way communication will drain more energy from LoraWan devices which are generally powered by batteries. Therefore, LoraWAN defines classes based on the energy consumption constraints of different end devices. Class A implements the basic set of features; Class B enables scheduled listening; Class C has bi-directional communication.

2.2   Rancher Kubernetes Engine

Rancher Kubernetes Engine (RKE) is one of the container management that can help deploy Kubernetes engine anywhere. Rancher also unites the Kubernetes clusters with centralized authentication, access, and observability [13]. Rancher also offers K3s as Lightweight Kubernetes. K3s has a small memory footprint or binary, which contains the components to run a cluster. To keep the size small, K3s replace etcd by another datastore with sqllite3.

2.3 Docker

Docker is a lightweight container system to support rapid deployment [11]. Docker relies on the Kernel of the host OS, increasing the performance and reducing the footprint. Docker supports process-level isolation, with two concepts from the Kernel that are used: namespace and Cgroup. The namespace will isolate the communications in the container so the container cannot interact with other containers. Cgroup is used to specify which computer resources the container should be able to access, such as a certain amount of RAM, CPU cores, file system access.

2.4 InfluxDB

InfluxdB is an open-source tool for time series data [10]. Influxdb supports developers because it has many features that can be used for IoT development. Some features of InfluxdB are 1. SQL style query Language where it is has commonly used by a developer, 2. Retention Policies: Influxdb uses retention policies to handle data retention periods, 3. Automatically. Continuous Queries; these features make run as a continuous query which essentially means telling InfluxDB to run a query in the background and compare it automatically, 4. HTTP API-2 endpoints.

3 System Design

In this study, we addressed questions dealing with the configuration of an edge cluster for monitoring water with an edge computing approach. We configured Rancher Kubernetes Engine (RKE), Lightweight Kubernetes, and LoraWAN to run on edge devices. This configuration uses to collect data from the water sensor and analyze the data in the edge device. In addition, Fish Tracking with YOLO4 was inferences in Jetson Devices uses Deepstream pipeline and bundled in a Docker container to test the configuration performance under the RKE. The illustration of the systems is in Fig. 1.

3.1 Edge Devices

Edge Devices consists of three devices: Jetson-NX, Jetson Nano, and Raspberry-Pi4. All edge devices are installed with Lightweight Kubernetes (K3S), Docker, and some apps to support the tasks, such as Node-Red, InfluxDb, MQTT, and Grafana. Moreover, all devices are linked to the Rancher Kubernetes engine. One of the tasks on edge devices is receiving data from water sensors. Data in the

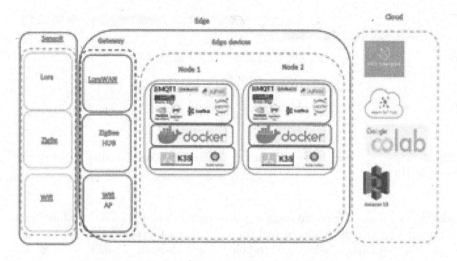

Fig. 1. Aquaculture monitoring system architecture.

database analyze to create a model prediction of Dissolved Oxygen Water. The tools to analyze data are Miniconda and JupyterLab, which are installed in the edged devices. In addition, to investigate the uses of GPU in the jetson devices, we implement Fish Tracking. Deepstream pipeline will use for maximizing the GPU in Jetson devices, an architecture. All apps that support the Edge server were a bundle in Docker and managed by K3s, and all devices will monitor in the Rancher.

3.2 Network

This system uses two kinds of network systems. The first system is to collect data from the sensors. Second, to coordinate from the cloud to the edge devices. LPWAN has been used to collect data from the sensor to the edge devices. Data from sensors will send using LoraWAN to the Lora Gateway. This network use Lora class A. For deploying an application in edge devices, we use RKE through the internet.

4 Experimental Results

4.1 Edge Devices

All the edge devices have been successfully installed with lightweight Kubernetes (K3s) and connected with Rancher Kubernetes Engine. Three devices use ARM-based processors, and one node was built using VMware ESXi as a comparison, as shown in Fig. 2. Then each device will deploy an application that is related to Intelligence Aquaculture. Data from the sensors will be managed with MQTT. Then with Node-Red, data will be filtered based on the classification and input

Fig. 2. Edge devices registered in rancher (A) and apps orchestration in every edge devices (B).

into the database. There are two databases Influxdb and MariaDB. Influxdb has a function to visualize data in real-time and has a function to set up the alert when the data has reached a threshold value. MariaDB is used to save data permanently and used to upload to the cloud. All applications deploy inside the Docker container. Another application that we try is real-time monitoring for fish detection on Jetson edge devices. We use the Nvidia Deepstream pipeline, which maximizes the GPU computation on Jetson devices [1]. Nvidia provides the Docker environment for Deepstream, so it can be applied on Lightweight Kubernetes (Fig. 3). The system used a camera to detect a fish in the Aquarium in real-time to test the Jetson device's performance [1]. The systems can identify a fish around 29 FPS. During real-time fish detection, the power consumption also rises around 8 W, wherein the idle condition is only about 3 W, as shown in Fig. 4. Fish detection builds using a YOLO4 and Deepsort [6]. A dataset for the trained model is available in mp4 format and converted into frames. The

Fig. 3. Real-time monitoring with DeepStream for fish detection.

extracted frames were then annotated using the LabelImg tool [9] with YOLO label format. All datasets are then Trained with Google Colab using GPU. The convolution filter size was selected as 21 × 21 since only two classes. The model then inferences to Jetson nano use DeepStream. All the process was coordinated using RKE. One of the advantages of using RKE is the availability of a matrix for the resources used. The matrix is used to monitor the resources of our edge devices. The edge devices have small resources, so it is crucial to observe the best conditions continuously.

4.2 Networks and Sensors

The Lora Gateway is set up in the lab of Tunghai University. In this experiment, we use an indoor Lora gateway. We use three sensors: Temperature, Dissolve Oxygen water, Conductivity, and pH water. We build water monitor systems with Arduino board as the main controlling board and use an expansion board to carry more sensors on the same board. All the sensors' readings will send to edge devices through the Lora gateway. MQTT then managed a message from Lora based on topics. Node-red then uses to insert data to InfluxDB and visualize. All data from the sensors were then visualized with InfluxDB. In addition, power consumption monitoring is also used to understand the number of power consumption when running the object detection and data analysis (Fig. 4).

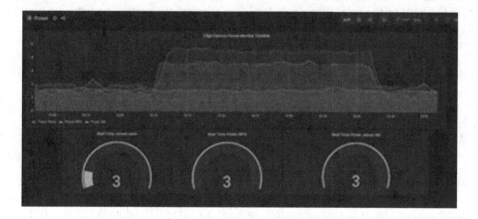

Fig. 4. Power consumption monitoring.

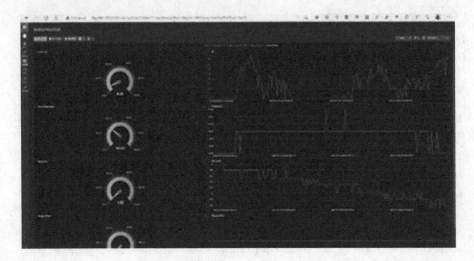

Fig. 5. A water sensor data collection

5 Discussion

The edge computing paradigm was run well in these systems. All edge nodes can collect data from sensors ideally. The graphic User Interface provided by RKE was easy to use and can help beginners deploy the system on edge devices. Ensure the installation process uses a correct RKE agent so that the edge devices can coordinate with the RKE servers (Fig. 5).

These systems collect not only data but also implement real-time fish detection. All tasks can run parallel and work perfectly. Deepstream pipeline optimizes the GPU on the edge devices for the video analytics process and only consumes less than 10 W. Unfortunately, RPI4 does not have GPU to process real-time video analytics, but we can use Movidius^{TM} Neural Compute Stick for AI inferencing.

6 Conclusion

Edge computing is a new paradigm in this era. There is much architecture to implement the Edge Computing. In this paper, we investigate the edge computing paradigm for implementing Intelligent Aquaculture. In this case, we emphasize real-time collecting data and fish detection. All systems must be based on containerization cause to help deployment proses of Intelligence Aquaculture system. Rancher Kubernetes Engine can fulfill our requirements, and Lightweight Kubernetes (K3s) can handle the artificial intelligence model bundles with Docker. Lightweight Kubernetes can maintain our model on the best performance. This architecture we will use to deploy our artificial intelligence model with the custom dataset in the future.

Acknowledgements. This work was supported by the Ministry of Science and Technology, Taiwan (R.O.C.), under grants number 110-2221-E-029-020-MY3 and 110-2811-E-029 -003.

References

1. Bakre, P.: I at the edge with K3s and Nvidia Jetson Nano: object detection and real-time video analytics (2021). https://www.suse.com/c/ai-at-the-edge-with-k3s-nvidia-jetson-nano-object-detection-real-time-video-analytics-src/. Accessed 16 Sept 2021
2. E.C. Consortium: Edge computing reference architecture 2.0 (2017). http://en.ecconsortium.net/Uploads/file/20180328/1522232376480704.pdf. Accessed 18 Sept 2021
3. Debauche, O., Mahmoudi, S., Mahmoudi, S.A., Manneback, P., Lebeau, F.: A new edge architecture for AI-IoT services deployment. Procedia Comput. Sci. **175**, 10–19 (2020)
4. Farmaki, E.G., et al.: Advanced multivariate techniques for the classification and pollution of marine sediments due to aquaculture. Sci. Total Environ. **763**, 144617 (2021)
5. Gupta, A., Mukherjee, N.: A cloudlet platform with virtual sensors for smart edge computing. IEEE Internet Things J. **6**(5), 8455–8462 (2019)
6. Liu, S., et al.: Embedded online fish detection and tracking system via YOLOv3 and parallel correlation filter. In: OCEANS 2018 MTS/IEEE Charleston, pp. 1–6. IEEE (2018)
7. Martínez-Casanueva, I.D., Bellido, L., Lentisco, C.M., Fernández, D.: An initial approach to a multi-access edge computing reference architecture implementation using Kubernetes. In: Gao, H., Durán Barroso, R.J., Shanchen, P., Li, R. (eds.) BROADNETS 2020. LNICST, vol. 355, pp. 185–193. Springer, Cham (2021). https://doi.org/10.1007/978-3-030-68737-3_13
8. Mondal, S.K., Pan, R., Kabir, H., Tian, T., Dai, H.N.: Kubernetes in it administration and serverless computing: an empirical study and research challenges. J. Supercomput. **78**, 2937–2987 (2021). https://doi.org/10.1007/s11227-021-03982-3
9. NaelsonDouglas: Labelimg (2021). https://github.com/tzutalin/labelImg. Accessed 16 Sept 2017
10. Nasar, M., Kausar, M.A.: Suitability of InfluxDB database for IoT applications. Int. J. Innov. Technol. Explor. Eng. **8**(10), 1850–1857 (2019)
11. Pääkkönen, P., Pakkala, D., Kiljander, J., Sarala, R.: Architecture for enabling edge inference via model transfer from cloud domain in a Kubernetes environment. Future Internet **13**(1), 5 (2021)
12. Queralta, J.P., Gia, T.N., Zou, Z., Tenhunen, H., Westerlund, T.: Comparative study of LPWAN technologies on unlicensed bands for M2M communication in the IoT: Beyond LoRa and LoRaWAN. Procedia Comput. Sci. **155**, 343–350 (2019)
13. Rancher: Kubernetes management for dummies (2021). https://rancher.com/. Accessed 26 Sept 2021
14. Yue, K., Shen, Y.: An overview of disruptive technologies for aquaculture. Aquacult. Fish. **7**, 111–120 (2021)
15. Zahmatkesh, H., Al-Turjman, F.: Fog computing for sustainable smart cities in the IoT era: caching techniques and enabling technologies-an overview. Sustain. Urban Areas **59**, 102139 (2020)

Design and Implementation of Water Monitoring Using LoRa and NB-IoT

Endah Kristiani[1,2], Chien-Yi Chen[1], Chao-Tung Yang[1,3]([ID]),
and Ti-Feng Hsieh[1]

[1] Department of Computer Science, Tunghai University, No. 1727, Sec. 4,
Taiwan Boulevard, Taichung 407224, Taiwan (R.O.C.)
ctyang@thu.edu.tw
[2] Department of Informatics, Krida Wacana Christian University,
Jakarta 11470, Indonesia
[3] Research Center for Smart Sustainable Circular Economy, Tunghai University,
No. 1727, Sec. 4, Taiwan Boulevard, Taichung 407224, Taiwan (R.O.C.)

Abstract. Array of Things in smart city initiatives can add tremendous value to the life of citizens and public servants alike by constructing apps that make use of disparate information streams. Data integration and visualization platforms can generate real situational awareness, measurable smart city a better quality of life for urban inhabitants by interpreting and reorganizing information from networks of devices integrated across towns. In this study, the implementation of Array of Things is demonstrated in water quality monitoring and analysis as the experimental study using LoRa and NB-IoT.

Keywords: AIOT · IoT · Water monitoring · NB-IoT

1 Introduction

The use of the right technologies in planning and working is one of the main ways to achieve a smart city. The harmony of the fundamental intelligent city objectives and goals must be linked to best digital technology and intelligent technology. Intelligent information must be used to transform a campus or town and use the finest technology. The maxims, analytics and heuristic algorithms behind the efficient use of intelligent information remain critical to any effort to build a better, safer and smarter city, where people and neighborhoods thrive, technology is deployed and people are employed in a profitable manner. In effectively analyzing and addressing technology, efficient planning, and intelligent details, it can lead to a sense of real society. This means that social cohesion is nurtured and smart procedures and efficient techniques can flourish all over the areas.

The Internet of Things (IoT) and Array of Things (AoT) provides cities with new opportunities to use the information to handle traffic, reduce pollution, make better use of infrastructure and maintain people secure. A fully integrated

Y.-B. Lin et al. (Eds.): SGIoT 2021, LNICST 447, pp. 46–52, 2022.
https://doi.org/10.1007/978-3-031-20398-5_5

modular and scalable framework to effectively deliver and handle smart city services to assist towns make the most of digital opportunities. The completely integrated strategy fulfills the essential necessity of a shared, secure, and scalable linked environment where every "thing" can communicate to each other to make the towns of tomorrow smart, secure, and viable.

In this paper, the implementation of IoT and AoT for smart city is demonstrated in water monitoring and analysis. The design system is deployed in the campus as a living labs.

2 Background Review and Related Study

In this section, we review some background knowledges for later use of system design and implementation. Several components are applied as the methods in this paper: IoT, Big Data, Cloud Computing, and OpenStack. The next parts discuss each component in more detail.

2.1 The Internet of Things (IoT)

The IoT is a network of physical machines, cars, home appliances, and other products integrated with electronics, software, sensors, actuators, and connectivity to the network that allows these objects to communicate and exchange information. Through its embedded computing scheme, each thing is uniquely recognizable but can interoperate within the current Internet infrastructure. Experts estimate that around 30 billion objects will consist of IoT by 2020.

The IoT enables objects to be sensed or remotely monitored across current network infrastructure, creating possibilities for more direct integration of the physical globe into computer-based systems, and resulting in enhanced effectiveness, precision, and financial benefits in relation to decreased human interference. When IoT is enhanced with sensors and actuators, the technology becomes an example of the more general class of cyber-physical devices, including technologies such as smart grids, virtual energy plants, smart homes, smart transportation and smart towns.

2.2 The Array of Things (AoT)

The Array of Things (AoT) is an urban sensing network of programmable and modular nodes to collect data on the city's climate, facilities, science and public use in real time in cities. AoT will primarily serve the community, as measurement of the living conditions in cities like the weather, air quality and noise.

AoT will provide researchers and the public with real-time location data on the urban environment, infrastructure and activity This initiative was structured so that scientists, policy-makers, developers and residents can collaborate and take specific measures to improve the security, productivity and well-being of cities. The data will help communities operate more efficiently and save on costs by predicting problems like air quality status and health.

2.3   NB-IoT

Narrow-band Internet of Things (NB-IoT) is a wide-area network communication system that uses a narrow band radio frequency. It operates inside the permitted spectrum. The licensing frequency band is used by 3GPP's 2/3/4G cellular communication technologies. Different from the existing networks, three deployment options such as in-band, guardband or independent carrier coexist, and NB-IoT is also supported by telecom firms throughout the world. A key LPWAN technology, as well as a leading solution for large-scale connectivity in all three of 5G's core use cases, is LoRA [6]. There is a 20 dB improvement in coverage capacity compared to LTE, which is comparable to a 100-fold increase in coverage area. Because of its deep coverage capabilities, it can also be used in industrial settings like factories, underground garages, and manhole covers. NB-IoT can enable 50–100 times more accesses than current wireless technologies on the same base station. It is possible for a sector to accommodate up to 100,000 connections while also providing low latency sensitivity, ultra-low equipment costs, low equipment power consumption, and a well-designed network architecture. NB-IoT network does not need to be rebuilt, and it saves money over LoRa because the radio frequency and antenna may be reused multiple times [7].

2.4   Related Study

The network architecture based on LoRaWAN is facing the problem of environmental limitations, and its harsh propagation environment greatly limits the coverage of the LoRaWAN network in the city. Dias and Grilo [2] designed and implemented a multi-hop uplink solution compatible with the LoRaWAN specification, which can be used as an extension to the deployed gateway. The terminal node transmits the data message to the intermediate node, and the intermediate node selects a route based on a simplified version of the target sequence distance vector (DSDV) routing and relays them to the gateway.

Celesti and Fazio [3] proposed an IoT system monitoring and management framework, which integrates the AllJoyn function, used to interconnect IoT devices, MongoDB, used to achieve big data storage, and Storm, used to run real-time data analysis. In the experiment, the author studied three different data modes, namely normal, event-based and automation. The experimental results show that the delay of monitoring and service depends largely on the type of management application running in the system, and is not affected by the data pattern.

Chen and Ran [1] proposed a smart city smart manhole cover management system based on edge computing in 2017; Wang et al. [4] designed a smart manhole cover management system based on multi-layer distributed structure and NB-IoT network in 2018. Smart street light management system for solar street lights; Zhang et al. [5] completed the long-range (LoRa) communication technology and the least recently used (LRU) algorithm to design a low-power information monitoring system in 2018; Anand and Regi [8] used NB-IoT to remotely monitor the water tank in 2018 The water level.

3   System Architecture

The overall architecture of this research is shown in Fig. 1. It is mainly composed of two parts. The first part is the hardware which includes Arduino deployment, water sensors, and combined with LoRa and NB-IoT modules, assembled into high-quality airboxes. The second part is the data source, collecting information of the water sensory data of Tunghai University. MySQL was used as the database system for sensory data. Grafana was applied to visualize the water monitoring system. The communication system uses MQTT transmissions. Figure 1 describes the system architecture of this research.

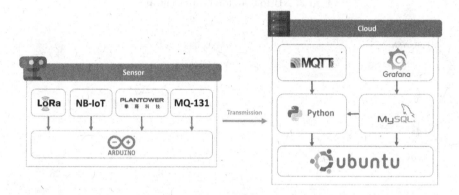

Fig. 1. Water monitoring system architecture

There are four layers in NB-IoT system, Perception, Transport, Platform, and Application layers. The architecture diagram of NB-IoT is shown in Fig. 2.

Transmit data quickly and save energy is also a major issue, therefore this system uses Message Queuing Telemetry Transport (MQTT) as a bridge of communication between machines. Figure 3 shows the scheme of overall data transmissions and System runtime process.

4   Experimental Results

4.1   Device Installation

The device is equipped with several sensors, including temperature sensor DS18b20, pH sensor, conductive sensor, and dissolved oxygen sensor. The sensing range of temperature is $-55\,°C$–$125\,°C$, the sensing range of pH is 0–14, the sensing range of conductivity is 1 ms/cm–20 ms/cm, and the sensing range of DO is 0–20 mg/L. A total of four values are obtained for LoRaWAN and MQTT transmission, which can operate normally regardless of indoor aquariums and outdoor lakes. Figure 4 presents the water sensor component.

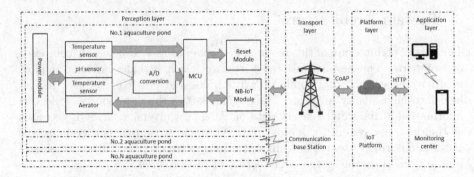

Fig. 2. NB-IoT architecture diagram

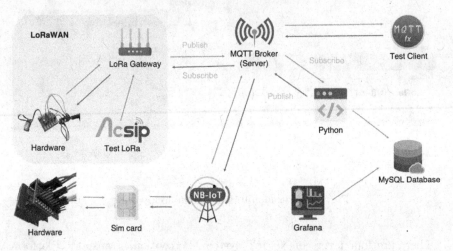

Fig. 3. System runtime process

4.2 Water Monitoring System

Grafana and WordPress were built to complete the tasks of data access and visualization. It is expected to present the real-time water status. WordPress was used to manage data access permissions and Web API interface to communicate with other sub-projects. The reason using Grafana because Grafana has the following six main features:

- Convenient display: Convenient and flexible graphical operations, and rich visual charts are available use.
- Multiple data sources: Many different data sources are supported.
- Early warning notification: Visually define the early warning rules for important indicators in the data.
- Mixed display: Different data sources can be mixed in the same chart, and combined display according to custom queries.

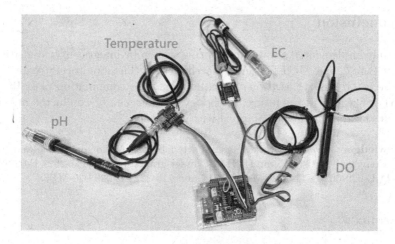

Fig. 4. Water sensor components

– Monitoring template: the old monitoring can be stored as a template, so that different hosts with the same data source can be quickly imported and applied.
– Permission control: You can control the access permissions of the underlying users by establishing different role permissions.

Figure 5 demonstrates the result of Water monitoring system in Grafana visualization.

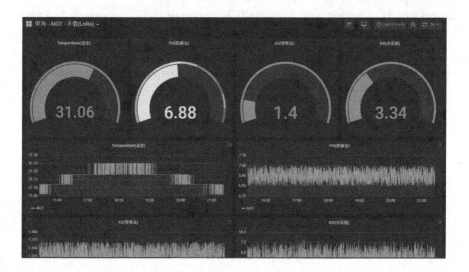

Fig. 5. Water monitoring in Grafana visualization

5 Conclusion

This study implemented a water monitoring system by integrating water sensors, LoRa, NB-IoT, and MQTT as AIOT architecture. The monitoring results then visualize in Grafana. Based on the experiment, the combination of LoRa and NB-IoT is feasible. In the future, further evaluations can be conducted in detail. Also, this system might be equipped with AI model.

Acknowledgement. This work was supported by the National Science and Technology Council (NSTC), Taiwan (R.O.C.), under grants number 111-2622-E-029-003-, 111-2811-E-029-001-, 111-2621-M-029-004-, and 110-2221-E-029-020-MY3.

References

1. Chen, J., Ran, X.: Deep learning with edge computing: a review. Proc. IEEE **107**(8), 6 (2019)
2. Dias, J., Grilo, A.: LoRaWAN multi-hop uplink extension. Procedia Comput. Sci. **130**, 424–431 (2018)
3. Celesti, A., Fazio, M.: A framework for real time end to end monitoring and big data oriented management of smart environments. J. Parallel Distrib. Comput. **132**, 262–273 (2018)
4. Wang, S., Zhao, Y., Xu, J., Yuan, J., Hsu, C.H.: Edge server placement in mobile edge computing. J. Parallel Distrib. Comput. **127**, 160–168 (2018)
5. Zhang, Y., Ren, J., Liu, J., Xu, C., Guo, H., Liu, Y.: A survey on emerging computing paradigms for big data. Chin. J. Electron. **26**(1), 1–12 (2017)
6. Dawaliby, S., Bradai, A., Pousset, Y.: Adaptive dynamic network slicing in LoRa networks. Future Gener. Comput. Syst. **98**, 697–707 (2019)
7. Loukatos, D., Manolopoulos, I., Arvaniti, E., Arvanitis, K.G., Sigrimis, N.A.: Experimental testbed for monitoring the energy requirements of LPWAN equipped sensor nodes. IFAC-PapersOnLine **51**(17), 309–313 (2018)
8. Anand, S., Regi, R.: Remote monitoring of water level in industrial storage tanks using NB-IoT. In: International Conference on Communication Information and Computing Technology (ICCICT) 2018, pp. 1–4 (2018). https://doi.org/10.1109/ICCICT.2018.8325871

InterWorking Function for Mission Critical Push to Talk Services

Chih-Cheng Tseng[1]([✉]), Shao-Yu Lien[2], Chuan-Xian Zhuang[1], Fang-Chang Kuo[1], and Hwang-Cheng Wang[1]

[1] National Ilan University, Yilan City, Taiwan
tsengcc@niu.edu.tw
[2] National Chung Cheng University, Chiayi, Taiwan

Abstract. Due to the continuous development of mobile communication technologies, commercialized mobile communication systems have been globally deployed. Among them, LTE-A (Long-Term Evolution-Advanced) has been adopted by several countries for the next generation PSNs (Public Safety Networks). To this end, 3GPP has also standardized Mission Critical Push To Talk (MCPTT) services in Release 13. Since the LMR (Land Mobile Radio) system has been widely adopted as the primary technology of the PSNs for a long time, it will take several years for LTE-A to replace it completely. Consequently, issues related to the interconnection of the LTE-A and LMR systems have received attention. In view of this, the interconnection of LTE-A and LMR systems has been standardized in 3GPP Release 15. A new function named IWF (InterWorking Function) was introduced to enable communications between LTE-A and LMR systems. Based on the considered system architecture, this paper first presents the implementation of IWF. Then, MCPTT group call for members between LTE-A and LMR systems is used to verify the feasibility and functionality of the implemented IWF.

Keywords: LTE-A · MCPTT · IWF · LMR

1 Introduction

1.1 Background

Land Mobile Radio (LMR) systems, including P25 (Project 25) [1] in North America and TETRA (TErrestrial Trunked RAdio) [2] in Europe, have been a legacy technology for public safety communications for decades. However, due to the advance of mobile broadband communication technologies in recent years, LTE-A (Long-Term Evolution-Advanced) system has been adopted for the next generation PSNs (Public Safety Networks) by several countries. Hence, it is estimated to take years for LTE-A system to replace the LMR system completely. Before this, it is expected that the LMR systems and the LTE-A based PSNs will coexist in the next couple of years. Consequently, inter-connectivity and interoperability between the LTE-A system and the LMR system have

Y.-B. Lin et al. (Eds.): SGIoT 2021, LNICST 447, pp. 53–68, 2022.
https://doi.org/10.1007/978-3-031-20398-5_6

become critical issues. To address these issues, 3GPP has standardized MCPTT services in Release 13 [3–5]. Furthermore, 3GPP formulated a standard for the interconnection between the MC (Mission Critical) system and the LMR system. It introduced a new function named IWF (InterWroking Function) in Release 15 [6] to specify the support for the interworking between the MC system and the LMR system under the requirements defined in [5] and [7]. In [6], the term *interworking* is defined as a means of communication between the MC system and the LMR system whereby MC users obtaining service from an MC system can communicate with LMR users obtaining service from one or more LMR systems.

1.2 Motivation

Considering that MC systems will coexist with the LMR systems for a period of time, the interconnection capability between devices in MC systems and LMR systems is necessary. There are platforms on the market that enable LTE-A devices and LMR devices to connect to each other [8, 9]. However, the cost of these existing platforms is not friendly. Therefore, this paper focuses on designing and implementing a cost-effective prototype platform of the IWF.

1.3 Goal and Contributions

Among the procedures specified in [6], the following are implemented in the IWF:

- Affiliation: Allow LMR users to join a selected group via IWF.
- De-affiliation: Allow LMR users to leave the selected group via IWF.
- Group call: Allow LMR users to make group calls with other members in the same group via IWF and vice versa.
- Floor control: Allow LMR users to request for the floor to make a group call.

2   The Design and Implementation of the IWF Prototype Platform

2.1 System Architecture

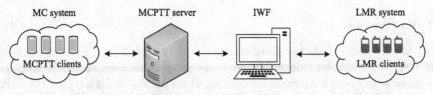

Fig. 1. System architecture

The design of the presented IWF is based on the considered system architecture (see Fig. 1). In this architecture, users in the MC system are identified by MC IDs. After authorization, they obtain MC service(s) and are regarded as MC users. Besides, users in the LMR system are regarded as LMR users. The main components of the architecture are the follows:

MC System: The MC system is defined as the collection of applications, services, and enabling capabilities required to provide a single MC service or multiple MC services to one or more MC organizations [10].

MCPTT Client: The MCPTT client is an App installed on a smartphone or pad. With the help of the installed App, the smartphone or pad provides the MCPTT services such as making group calls with other members in the same group with the help of the MCPTT server and IWF.

MCPTT Server: The MCPTT server is installed in a linux-based OS (Operating System) and is responsible for providing MCPTT services to the authenticated clients (MCPTT clients and IWF).

IWF: IN [6], IWF is defined as an entity that *"Adapts LMR systems to MC systems via the IWF interface and supports interworking between LMR systems and MC systems."* Besides, IWF is required to support necessary protocol translation and identity mapping between the MC systems and the LMR systems. Thus, IWF can be regarded as the representative of LMR clients in the MC system. The presented IWF prototype platform is implemented in Java and is operated in a linux-based OS.

LMR System: The LMR system is the collection of applications, services, and enabling capabilities for providing LMR service of group and private communications [6].

LMR Client: The LMR client is the radio operated by an LMR user and is capable of using the MCPTT services such as making group calls with other members in the same group in the MC system with the help of the MCPTT server and IWF.

2.2 Related Protocols

The protocols of IWF can be divided into control-plane and user-plane protocols. Control plane-related protocols are based on TCP (Transmission Control Protocol) and include SIP (Session Initiation Protocol), SDP (Session Description Protocol), and HTTP (Hypertext Transfer Protocol). User plane-related protocols are based on UDP (User Datagram Protocol) and include RTP and RTCP.

SIP: SIP [11] is an application layer protocol based on TCP or UDP. SIP provides a variety of request methods (see Table 1) and response codes (see Table 2), which make it suitable for establishing, modifying, and terminating media sessions.

SDP: SDP [12] is used to negotiate the establishment of a multimedia data traffic channel between caller and callee. During the three-way handshake process of the SIP INVITE request, SDP is used to exchange the media parameters between the two endpoints.

HTTP: HTTP [13] is an application layer protocol. HTTP functions as a request-response protocol in the client-server model. In the considered system architecture, HTTP is used to get user profile and group information, such as the list of all groups in the MCPTT server.

Table 1. SIP request methods

Method	Description
REGISTER	Register the user's URI
INVITE	Establish session
ACK	Confirm that an entity has received a final response to an INVITE request
BYE	Release session
CANCEL	Cancel any pending request
UPDATE	Modify the information of a session
REFER	Ask the recipient to issue a request for the purpose of call transfer
PRACK	Provisional acknowledgment
SUBSCRIBE	Initiate a subscription for notification of events from a notifier
NOTIFY	Inform a subscriber of notifications of a new event
PUBLISH	Publish an event to a notification server
MESSAGE	Deliver a text message
INFO	Send mid-session information
OPTIONS	Query the capabilities of an endpoint

Table 2. SIP response codes

Result	Description
1xx	Provisional response to request indicating the request is valid and is being processed
2xx	Successful completion of the request
3xx	Call redirection is needed for the completion of the request
4xx	Client error: The request cannot be completed
5xx	Server error: The server fails to fulfill an apparently valid request
6xx	Global error: The request cannot be fulfilled at any server

RTCP: RTCP [14] is a UDP-based application layer protocol. The primary function of RTCP is to provide feedback on the QoS (Quality of Service) in media distribution by periodically sending statistical information such as transmitted octet and packet counts. Moreover, in 3GPP TS24.380, RTCP is adopted to implement floor control.

RTP: RTP [14] is a UDP-based application layer protocol designed exclusively for end-to-end and real-time transfer of streaming media.

3 Group Configuration Procedures

To enable LMR clients to communicate with MCPTT clients, as the representative of the LMR clients, IWF is required to affiliate to the same group as the MCPTT clients. The procedures for IWF to affiliate and de-affiliate to a group are presented below. Based on the procedures, IWF exchanges all the required messages with the MCPTT server. In this way, we ensure that all the group-related messages can be validated by the MCPTT server.

3.1 Requesting the List of Existing Groups

Before proceeding with the affiliation procedures, IWF needs to know the existing groups in the MCPTT server. To this end, the request to obtain the latest group list is embedded in the command field of the HTTP GET request. Details of this procedure are illustrated in Fig. 2 and described below.

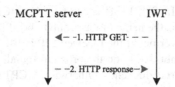

Fig. 2. Procedures to request for the list of existing groups

Step 1: To request the list of all groups that currently exist in the MCPTT server, IWF sends an HTTP GET request to the MCPTT server.

Step 2: After parsing the contents in the command field of the received HTTP GET request and verifying it as requesting for the list of existing groups, the MCPTT server replies with an HTTP response in which the latest list of all existing groups in the MCPTT server is included.

3.2 Requesting the List of Affiliated Groups

To know the groups that have been affiliated, IWF uses a procedure similar to that for requesting the list of existing groups to exchange messages with the MCPTT server. The request to obtain the list of affiliated groups is embedded in the command field of the HTTP GET request. Details of this procedure are described below.

Step 1: To request the list of groups that have been affiliated, IWF sends an HTTP GET request to the MCPTT server.

Step 2: After parsing the contents in the command field of the received HTTP GET request and verifying it as requesting for the list of affiliated groups, the MCPTT server replies with an HTTP response in which the list of groups that have been affiliated is included.

3.3 Affiliation

To affiliate to a group, IWF first selects a group that has not been affiliated. After that, IWF proceeds to execute the affiliation procedure as depicted in Fig. 3 to affiliate to the selected group. Details of this procedure are described below.

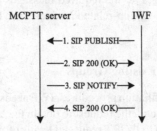

MCPTT server   IWF

←—1. SIP PUBLISH—
—2. SIP 200 (OK)—→
—3. SIP NOTIFY—→
←—4. SIP 200 (OK)—

Fig. 3. Affiliation/De-affiliation procedure [3, 6]

Step 1: IWF sends a SIP PUBLISH request to the MCPTT server in which the required information, such as the name of the group to be affiliated, is included.

Step 2: MCPTT server verifies if the received SIP PUBLISH request is sent by an authorized user of IWF. If not, based on the problem found, a corresponding SIP 4xx response is replied and the procedure ends. Otherwise, MCPTT server replies with a SIP 200 (OK) response and goes to Step 3.

Step 3: MCPTT server processes the information carried in SIP PUBLISH request and sends a SIP NOTIFY request to the IWF as the notification of the affiliation result. The possible status code of affiliation is 1, 3, 4, or 6, as shown in Table 3.

Step 4: IWF replies with a SIP 200 (OK) response after correctly receiving the SIP NOTIFY request.

Note that to make a group call, IWF is required to affiliate to that group first.

Table 3. Result of affiliation/de-affiliation

Status	Description
1	The result of affiliation is successful
2	The result of de-affiliation is successful
3	The number of group members exceeds the upper limit
4	The selected group has been affiliated before
5	The selected group has not been affiliated yet
6	The selected group does not exist
7	The number of group members cannot be less than two

3.4 De-affiliation

The administrator of IWF may want to de-affiliate a group from the list of affiliated groups. In this case, the IWF executes the same procedure as it does for affiliation in Fig. 3. Details of this procedure are described below.

Step 1: IWF sends a SIP PUBLISH request to the MCPTT server in which the required information, such as the name of the group that wants to be de-affiliated, is included.

Step 2: MCPTT server verifies if the received SIP PUBLISH request is sent by an authorized user of IWF. If not, based on the problem found, a corresponding SIP 4xx response is replied and the procedure ends. Otherwise, the MCPTT server replies with a SIP 200 (OK) response and goes to Step 3.

Step 3: MCPTT server processes the information carried in SIP PUBLISH request and sends a SIP NOTIFY request to the IWF as the notification of the de-affiliation result. The possible status code of de-affiliation is 2, 5, 6, or 7, as shown in Table 3.

Step 4: IWF replies with a SIP 200 (OK) response after correctly receiving the SIP NOTIFY request.

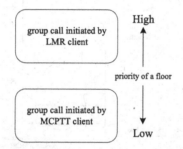

Fig. 4. Priority of a floor in the system

4 Floor Control

The members in a group can be classified as MCPTT clients and LMR clients. Consider the scenario in which an LMR client and an MCPTT client want to initiate a group call simultaneously and the LMR client successfully obtains the wireless channel to send voice messages. On receiving the voice messages, IWF sends a Floor Request message to the MCPTT server to request the floor for the LMR client. Similarly, the MCPTT client also sends a Floor Request message to the MCPTT server. Since the LMR client is operated in the half-duplex mode, it cannot transmit and receive messages simultaneously. If the MCPTT server grants the floor to the MCPTT client, there is no way to notify the LMR client that is currently in transmitting mode about this. Hence, the LMR client would not stop sending voice messages. Besides, all the voice messages from the LMR client will not be forwarded to the MCPTT clients. Although the floor is granted to the MCPTT client, IWF cannot forward all the voice messages from the

MCPTT client to the LMR client that is currently in transmitting mode. Therefore, when initiating a group call, the priority of the floor requested by the LMR client is higher than that by the MCPTT client of the same group to avoid the above problem The priority of a floor in the implemented system is shown in Fig. 4.

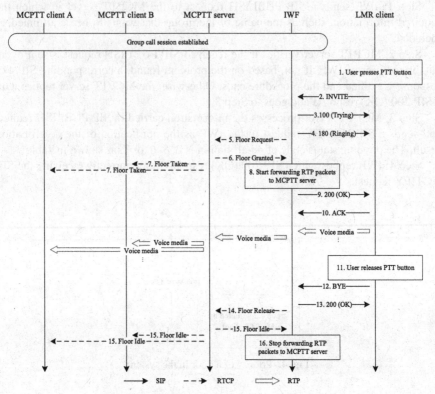

Fig. 5. LMR user initiates group call [6, 15]

5   Procedures for Initiating Group Call

5.1   LMR User Initiates Group Call

When an LMR user wants to make a group call, the following procedure will be performed (see Fig. 5).

Step 1: LMR user presses the PTT (Push To Talk) button to make a group call.

Step 2: After receiving the event that the PTT button is pressed, the LMR client sends a SIP INVITE request to the IWF.

Step 3: After successfully receiving the SIP INVITE request, IWF replies with a SIP 100 (Trying) response to the LMR client.

Step 4: IWF replies with a SIP 180 (Ringing) response notifying the LMR client that the media parameters carried in the SIP INVITE request are being processed.

Step 5: IWF sends a Floor Request message to the MCPTT server.

Step 6: After receiving the Floor Request, based on the priority of the request (see Fig. 4), the MCPTT server responds with a Floor Granted message to the IWF.

Step 7: The MCPTT server sends a Floor Taken message to the other members in the group call to notify them that IWF obtains the floor.

Step 8: After receiving the Floor Granted message, IWF enables the function of forwarding RTP packets to forward RTP packets from the LMR client to the MCPTT server.

Step 9: IWF includes its media parameters in a SIP 200 (OK) and sends the SIP 200 (OK) to the LMR client.

Step 10: After receiving the SIP 200 (OK) response, the LMR client analyzes and stores the media parameters carried in the SIP 200 (OK) response and replies with a SIP ACK to IWF.

After Step 10, the RTP packets generated by the LMR client are forwarded hop-by-hop to the other two group members, MCPTT clients A and B, in the MC system.

Step 11: LMR user releases the PTT button to terminate this group call.

Step 12: After receiving the event that the PTT button is released, the LMR client sends a SIP BYE request to the IWF.

Step 13: After receiving the SIP BYE request, IWF first replies with a SIP 200 (OK) to the LMR client. Then, IWF deletes the connection to the LMR client.

Step 14: IWF sends a Floor Release message to the MCPTT server to release the floor.

Step 15: After receiving the Floor Release message, the MCPTT server sends a Floor Idle message to all group members in this group call.

Step 16: After receiving the Floor Idle message, IWF disables the function of forwarding RTP packets to stop sending RTP packets from the LMR client to the MCPTT server.

5.2 MC User Initiates Group Call

When the MC user of MCPTT client A wants to make a group call, the following procedure will be performed (see).

Step 1: MC user presses the PTT button to make a group call.

Step 2: After receiving the event that the PTT button is pressed, MCPTT client A sends a Floor Request to the MCPTT server.

Step 3: Since only the Floor Request from MCPTT client A is received, based on the priority of the floor (see), the MCPTT server responds with a Floor Granted message to the MCPTT client A.

Step 4: The MCPTT server sends a Floor Taken message to other members participating in this group call to notify that MCPTT client A obtains the floor.

Step 5: After receiving the Floor Taken message, IWF sends a SIP INVITE request to the LMR client.

Step 6: After receiving the SIP INVITE request, the LMR client replies with a SIP 100 (Trying) response.

Step 7: LMR client continues to reply with a SIP 183 (Session Progress) response notifying IWF that the media parameters in the SIP INVITE request are being processed.

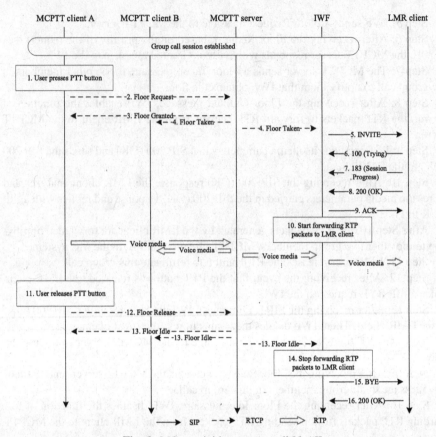

Fig. 6. MC user initiates group call [6, 15]

Step 8: LMR client includes its media parameters in a SIP 200 (OK) and replies with the SIP 200 (OK) to the IWF.

Step 9: After receiving the SIP 200 (OK) response, IWF analyzes and stores the media parameters carried in the SIP 200 (OK) response and replies with a SIP ACK to the LMR client.

Step 10: IWF enables the function of forwarding RTP packets and sends the RTP packets from the MCPTT server to the LMR client.

Step 11: MC user releases the PTT button to terminate this group call.

Step 12: After receiving the event that the PTT button is released, MCPTT client A forwards a Floor Release message to the MCPTT server.

Step 13: After receiving the Floor Release message, the MCPTT server sends a Floor Idle message to all group members participating in this group call.

Step 14: After receiving the Floor Idle message, IWF disables the function of forwarding RTP packets and stops sending RTP packets from the MCPTT server to the LMR client.

Step 15: IWF sends a SIP BYE request to the LMR client.

Step 16: After receiving the SIP BYE request, the LMR client replies with a SIP 200 (OK) and then deletes the connection with IWF.

6 Verification of the Implemented Procedures

Wireshark [16] was used to capture the exchanged packets while performing each of the procedures mentioned above for the verification of the procedures in the following use cases.

6.1 Group Configuration

Requesting the List of Existing Groups. The detailed description of the use case of requesting the list of existing groups and the corresponding captured packets are shown in Table 4 and Fig. 7, respectively. By comparing Fig. 2 with Fig. 7, we see that all the packets involved in the procedure for requesting the list of existing groups are correctly exchanged. Hence, the procedure for requesting the list of existing groups is verified.

Table 4. Use case of requesting the list of existing groups

Requesting the list of existing groups	
Description	The IWF requests the list of existing groups in the MCPTT server
Participants	MCPTT server and IWF
Post-conditions	The IWF obtains the list of existing groups
Note: IP address of the MCPTT server is 140.123.102.114 and IP address of IWF is 120.101.9.174	

Source	Destination	Protocol	Length	Info
120.101.9.174	140.123.102.114	HTTP	236	GET /restcomm/?cmd=GetAllGroupList HTTP/1.1
140.123.102.114	120.101.9.174	HTTP	60	HTTP/1.1 200 OK (text/plain)

Fig. 7. Captured packets for requesting the list of existing groups

Table 5. Use case of requesting the list of affiliated groups

Requesting the list of affiliated groups	
Description	The IWF requests the list of affiliated groups from the MCPTT server
Participants	MCPTT server and IWF
Post-conditions	The IWF obtains the list of affiliated groups
Note: IP addresses of MCPTT server and IWF are 140.123.102.114 and 120.101.9.174, respectively	

Requesting the List of Affiliated Groups. The detailed description of the use case of requesting the list of affiliated groups and the corresponding captured packets are shown in Table 5 and Fig. 8, respectively. Comparison of Fig. 2 and Fig. 8 reveals that all the required packets concerning the procedure for requesting the list of affiliated groups are correctly exchanged. Hence, the procedure for requesting the list of affiliated groups is verified.

Source	Destination	Protocol	Length	Info
120.101.9.174	140.123.102.114	HTTP	352	GET /restcomm/?cmd=GetData&Parm=140.123.102.114:15060/xcap-root
140.123.102.114	120.101.9.174	HTTP/XML	60	HTTP/1.1 200 OK

Fig. 8. Captured packets for requesting the list of affiliated groups

Table 6. Use case of affiliation

Affiliation	
Description	According to the list of existing groups, user selects one to affiliate. After the group is selected, IWF executes the affiliation procedure
Participants	MCPTT server and IWF
Post-conditions	According to the result included in the SIP NOTIFY request (see **Table 3**), IWF knows if it has successfully been affiliated to the selected group

Source	Destination	Protocol	Length	Info
120.101.9.174	140.123.102.114	SIP/XML	1506	Request: PUBLISH sip:EMCard31@140.123.102.114 | (application/vnd.3gpp.mcptt-info+xml)
140.123.102.114	120.101.9.174	SIP	344	Status: 200 OK |
140.123.102.114	120.101.9.174	SIP/XML	969	Request: NOTIFY sip:EMCard31@120.101.9.174:1434;transport=tcp |
120.101.9.174	140.123.102.114	SIP	441	Status: 200 OK |

Fig. 9. Captured packets for affiliating to the selected group

Affiliation. The detailed description of the use case of affiliation and the corresponding captured packets are shown in Table 6 and Fig. 9, respectively. From Fig. 3 and Fig. 9, it is clear that all the packets required by the procedure for affiliation are correctly exchanged. Hence, the procedure for affiliation is verified.

Table 7. Use case of de-affiliation

De-affiliation	
Description	According to the list of affiliated groups, user selects one to de-affiliate. After the group is selected, IWF executes the de-affiliation procedure
Participants	MCPTT server and IWF
Post-conditions	According to the result included in the SIP NOTIFY request (see Table 3), IWF knows if the selected group has successfully been de-affiliated

Source	Destination	Protocol	Length Info
120.101.9.174	140.123.102.114	SIP/XML	1500 Request: PUBLISH sip:EMCard31@140.123.102.114	(application/vnd.3gpp.mcptt-info+xml)
140.123.102.114	120.101.9.174	SIP	344 Status: 200 OK	
140.123.102.114	120.101.9.174	SIP/XML	972 Request: NOTIFY sip:EMCard31@120.101.9.174:1434;transport=tcp	
120.101.9.174	140.123.102.114	SIP	441 Status: 200 OK	

Fig. 10. Captured packets for de-affiliating the selected group

De-affiliation. The detailed description of the use case of de-affiliation and the corresponding captured packets are shown in Table 7 and Fig. 10, respectively. Comparion of Fig. 3 and Fig. 10 shows that all the required packets in the procedure for de-affiliation are correctly exchanged. Hence, the procedure for de-affiliation is verified.

6.2 LMR User Initiating Group Call

The detailed description of the use case of an LMR user initiating a group call is listed in Table 8, while the corresponding captured packets are shown in Fig. 11, Fig. 12, Fig. 13, and Fig. 14, respectively. Results in Fig. 11, Fig. 12, Fig. 13, and Fig. 14 indicate that all the required packets (see Fig. 5) in the procedure for an LMR user to initiate a group call are correctly exchanged. Hence, the the correctness of procedure is verified.

Table 8. Use case of LMR user initiating group call

LMR user initiates group call	
Description	The LMR user wants to initiate a group call
Participants	MCPTT server and IWF
Post-conditions	The RTP packets of the LMR client are forwarded by the IWF and the MCPTT server to the other group members in this group call

Note: Note: IP addresses of MCPTT server and IWF are 140.123.102.114 and 120.101.9.174, respectively. Private IP addresses of LMR client and IWF are 192.168.28.151 and 192.168.28.1, respectively

Source	Destination	Protocol	Length Info
192.168.28.151	192.168.28.1	SIP/SDP	889 Request: INVITE sip:402@192.168.28.1	
192.168.28.1	192.168.28.151	SIP	416 Status: 100 Trying	
192.168.28.1	192.168.28.151	SIP	416 Status: 180 Ringing	
192.168.28.1	192.168.28.151	SIP/SDP	774 Status: 200 OK	
192.168.28.151	192.168.28.1	SIP	388 Request: ACK sip:407@192.168.28.1	

Fig. 11. Captured packets for LMR client to establish a session to IWF

Source	Destination	Protocol	Length Info
120.101.9.174	140.123.102.114	RTCP	94 (MCPT) Floor Request[Malformed Packet]
140.123.102.114	120.101.9.174	RTCP	74 (MCPT) Floor Granted[Malformed Packet]

Fig. 12. Captured packets for IWF to obtain the floor

Source	Destination	Protocol	Length	Info
120.101.9.174	140.123.102.114	RTCP	90	(MCPT) Floor Release[Malformed Packet]
140.123.102.114	120.101.9.174	RTCP	62	(MCPT) Floor Idle[Malformed Packet]

Fig. 13. Captured packets for IWF to release the floor

Source	Destination	Protocol	Length	Info
192.168.28.151	192.168.28.1	SIP	389	Request: BYE sip:402@192.168.28.1 |
192.168.28.1	192.168.28.151	SIP	365	Status: 200 OK |

Fig. 14. Captured packets for LMR client to release a session to IWF

6.3   MC User Initiating Group Call

The detailed description of the use case of an MC user initiating a group call is listed in Table 9, while the corresponding captured packets are shown in Fig. 15, Fig. 16, Fig. 17, and Fig. 18, respectively. These figures show that all the required packets, as depicted in Fig. 6 in the procedure for an MC user to initiate a group call, are correctly exchanged. Hence, the correctness of the procedure is verified.

Table 9. Use case of MC user initiating group call

LMR user initiates group call	
Description	The MC user wants to initiate a group call
Participants	MCPTT server and IWF
Post-conditions	The RTP packets of MCPTT client are forwarded by the MCPTT server and the IWF to other group members in this group call

Note: Note: IP addresses of MCPTT server and IWF are 140.123.102.114 and 120.101.9.174, respectively. Private IP addresses of LMR client and IWF are 192.168.28.151 and 192.168.28.1, respectively

Source	Destination	Protocol	Length	Info
140.123.102.114	120.101.9.174	RTCP	106	(MCPT) Floor Taken[Malformed Packet]

Fig. 15. Captured packet for IWF to be informed about the floor has been taken

Source	Destination	Protocol	Length	Info
192.168.28.1	192.168.28.151	SIP/SDP	888	Request: INVITE sip:407@192.168.28.151 |
192.168.28.151	192.168.28.1	SIP	415	Status: 100 Trying |
192.168.28.151	192.168.28.1	SIP	416	Status: 180 Ringing |
192.168.28.151	192.168.28.1	SIP/SDP	787	Status: 200 OK |
192.168.28.1	192.168.28.151	SIP	372	Request: ACK sip:407@192.168.28.151 |

Fig. 16. Captured packets for IWF to establish a session to the LMR client

Source	Destination	Protocol	Length	Info
140.123.102.114	120.101.9.174	RTCP	62	(MCPT) Floor Idle[Malformed Packet] ˙

Fig. 17. Captured packet for IWF to be informed about the floor is idle

Source	Destination	Protocol	Length	Info
192.168.28.1	192.168.28.151	SIP	372	Request: BYE sip:407@192.168.28.151 |
192.168.28.151	192.168.28.1	SIP	361	Status: 200 OK |

Fig. 18. Captured packets for IWF to release the session to LMR client

7 Conclusion

To achieve the interworking between MC systems and LMR systems, IWF was standardized by the 3GPP. Based on the standardized IWF and the considered system architecture, a simplified IWF prototype platform has been implemented based on the six considered use cases: Requesting The List of Existing Groups, Requesting The List of Affiliated Groups, Affiliation, De-affiliation, LMR User Initiating Group Call, and MC User Initiating Group Call. Procedures for the six considered use cases have been developed. We used Wireshark to capture the packets exchanged to verify the operability and applicability of the developed procedures. Carefully comparing the developed procedures and the captured packets confirmed the operability and applicability of the six use cases. In addition to further increasing the MCPTT use cases for the implemented IWF prototype platform, we intend to support more MC services (e.g., MCData [7] and MCVideo [17]) in the future.

Acknowledgment. This work was supported in part by the Ministry of Science and Technology, Taiwan, R. O. C., under grant number MOST 109–2221-E-197–028-MY3.

References

1. APCO: "Project 25 Push-to-X" website, https://www.apcointl.org/spectrum-management/spectrum-management-resources/interoperability/p25/. Last accessed 30 August 2021
2. ETSI: "TErrestrial Trunked RAdio" website, https://www.etsi.org/technologies/tetra. Last accessed 30 August 2021
3. 3GPP: Functional architecture and information flows to support Mission Critical Push to Talk (MCPTT), TS 23.379 (July 2020)
4. 3GPP: Mission Critical Push to Talk (MCPTT) call control (Release 16), TS 24.379 (June 2021)
5. 3GPP: Mission Critical Push to Talk over LTE requirements (Release 16), TS 22.179 (March 2019)
6. 3GPP: Mission Critical Communication Interworking with Land Mobile Radio Systems (Release 16), TS 23.283 (Sept 2020)
7. 3GPP: Mission Critical Data over LTE (Release 14), TS 22.282 (March 2017)
8. SAMSUNG: "Solving Critical Communication Challenges with Mission Critical Push-to-X" website, https://images.samsung.com/is/content/samsung/assets/global/business/networks/insights/white-paper/samsung-mcptx/Samsung_MCPTX_SolutionBrief_FINAL_r1.pdf. Last accessed 22 August 2021

9. Catalyst: "Interworking - Catalyst Communication Technologies" website, https://www.cat comtec.com/technology/lmr-lte-interworking/. Last accessed 22 August 2021
10. 3GPP: Common Functional Architecture to Support Mission Critical Services (Release 17), TS 23.280 (June 2021)
11. Rosenberg, J. et al.: SIP: Session Initiation Protocol, RFC 3261 (June 2002)
12. Handley, M., Mark, V.J., Perkins, C.: SDP: Session Description Protocol, RFC 4566 (July 2006)
13. Fielding, R., et al.: Hypertext Transfer Protocol -- HTTP/1.1, RFC 2616 (June 1999)
14. Schulzrinne, H., Casner, S., Frederick, R., Jacobson, V.: RTP: A Transport Protocol for Real-Time Applications, RFC 3550 (July 2003)
15. 3GPP: Technical Specification Group Core Network and Terminals Mission Critical Push To Talk (MCPTT) media plane control, TS 24.380 (Dec. 2019)
16. Wireshark: https://www.wireshark.org/. Last accessed 22 August 2021
17. 3GPP: Mission Critical Video over LTE (Release 14), TS 22.281 (March 2017)

Communication Security, Big Data, Neural Networks and Machine Learning

Lightweight Privacy-Preserving Data Aggregation Scheme Based on Elliptic Curve Cryptography for Smart Grid Communications

Thokozani Felix Vallent[1]([⊠])[iD], Damien Hanyurwimfura[1][iD],
Jayavel Kayalvizhi[2][iD], Hyunsung Kim[3,4][iD], and Chomora Mikeka[5][iD]

[1] College of Science and Technology, African Center of Excellence in Internet
of Things (ACEIoT), University of Rwanda, KN Street Nyarugenge,
P.O. Box 3900, Kigali, Rwanda
tfvallent@gmail.com, dhanyurwimfura@ur.ac.rw

[2] School of Computing, Department of Information Technology, SRM Institute of
Science and Technology, Potheri, Kattankulathur Campus, Chennai, India
kayalvij@srmist.edu.in

[3] School of Computer Science, Kyungil University, Gyeongsan-si, South Korea
kim@kiu.kr

[4] Chancellor College, Mathematical Science Department,
University of Malawi, P.O. Box 280, Zomba, Malawi

[5] Chancellor College, Department of Physics, University of Malawi,
P.O. Box 280, Zomba, Malawi
cmikeka@cc.ac.mw

Abstract. Smart grid (SG) is a modern electricity grid based on bi-directional flow of electricity and information for efficient energy management. Due to dependence on information communication, the system is prone to potential cyber-security attacks such as, user identity theft and data privacy breach. Addressing these cyber-security issues with optimal efficiency in smart grid is an open research problem. From this perspective this paper proposes a lightweight scheme for robust information security and privacy-preservation in data aggregation in SG. The proposed scheme utilizes elliptic curve variant of El Gamal encryption cryptosystem and signcryption techniques to achieve user anonymity with greater efficiency. The scheme satisfies the standard security requirements proven in the random oracle model and does not need a trusted third-party or certificate issuance during scheme run. Performance evaluation analysis shows that the proposed scheme has a better overall performance to most relevant comparable schemes, since it does not use heavy computation operations such as bilinear pairings, map-to-point hash operations, exponentiation among others. Furthermore, the proposed scheme does not depend on trusted authority (TA) neither suffers from coalition attack nor insider attacks.

Supported by University of Rwanda.

Keywords: Smart grid · Data aggregation · Bi-directional communication · Elliptic curve cryptography · Internet of things · Privacy-preserving

1   Introduction

As the future power grid, smart grid (SG) surpasses the legacy grid with a greater advantage due to incorporation of advanced communication technology in the electricity system [5,13,14,42,50,59]. In accordance to the model of National Institute of Standards and technology (NIST), smart meter (SM) based at the residential area collects and sends real-time electricity usage data to the operation center (OC), and in a similar manner a SM receives command messages related to control and management of electricity from OC [26]. In SG the electricity data bears economic value as it can be used for electricity marketing, management and regulation in applications such as demand response [20,24,30]. An existing challenge with the electricity consumer's consumption data is that it contains privacy information such that it can reveal the user's identification, lifestyle pattern and habits of electricity usage of the consumers, which is not a desirable thing [6,10,15,54,60].

In SG, recording of power consumption data is done not on month-to-month basis as is the case with the legacy grid, but rather is based on times of the day and gives details of the power consumption of individual appliances on the customers side in near real-time intervals [48,65]. On the negative note this detailed information has a potential of being used maliciously by an attacker to invade privacy and security. For instance, by knowing the times house owners' sleep or are absent from home based on analysis of SM information flow, thieves can plan to break into the homes when nobody is at home. Hence there is great need to protect the consumer's side against privacy and security breaches associated with smart meter information, with respect to the basic security requirements. That is to ensure SM communications should be supported with user authentication and identification measures when transacting on the open network between the SM and the monitoring device. Encryption with efficient algorithm for the customer consumption information transmitted by the SM to the utility or third party service providers will also be needed. The communication scheme should also protect individual energy consumer information from third parties for commercial purposes not related to services provided by the utility that is the scheme should be resilient to all sort of insider attacks [67].

However, the current challenge is ensuring security and privacy of smart grid AMI communications and balancing between lightweight cryptographic measures and ideal computational complexity for resource constrained devices. Once lightweight privacy-preserving and security mechanism are ascertained, consumers and utility are likely to have a widely varying preferences on how they wish to control and monitor third party to access their information. Thus, the challenge to protect user's privacy information effectively and efficiently has attracted researchers attention to find a lasting solution [8,34,39,67,70]. Such solutions would ensure the adoption of internet of things(IoT) applications over smart grid, since they consist of resource-constrained devices. Privacy-preserving data aggregation approach is one of viable mechanisms feasible for achieving data privacy [9,56,71]. Privacy-protection safeguards the fine-grained user data from disclosure to unwanted parties like the gateway or the system service provider during transmission and in some cases even protected from insider attack within the control center itself. Data aggregation is an ideal solution for securing data from eavesdroppers and has the advantage of improving network performance by virtue of reducing communication traffic. This approach goes with the following requirements: 1) the data aggregation operator can obtain of usage data in a region; 2) the data aggregation operator should know nothing about individual usage data in the data collection region [36,40,45].

In this regard, homomorphic encryption (HE) is a prospective mechanism for ensuring data aggregation privacy because it allows ciphertext manipulation without divulging plain-text [51]. The HE technique allows performing of addition operation or multiplication operation on encrypted cipher without requiring decryption, which is the desirable property for the aggregation operator to do, since it is a semi-trusted entity. There are several other data aggregation techniques such as using random numbers secrete sharing, Boneh-Goh-Nissim homomorphic encryption, Paillier homomorphic encryption, data slicing, differential privacy among other techniques [4]. In random number secret sharing design a series of random numbers with underlying properties are initially distributed to all the entities in the network that is to, all users and the data aggregation operators in advance, which are later used to obfuscate the usage data transmitted in the network [32]. The drawback of such a mechanism is reliance on Trusted Third Party (TTP) responsible for generating and distributing such random numbers. Differential privacy is also a technique for achieving privacy which adds random noise of Laplacian distribution or other distributions to mask the original value [17]. However, in many studies, this technique of differential privacy is deemed less accurate. Secret sharing which was proposed by Shamir in [55], is also another mechanism used to achieve privacy data aggregation. In this method group secret is split into shares and distributed amongst the participants and each one is kept highly confidential. The secret can only be reconstructed with a sufficient number of participants colluding and combining their secret values together, as such it is good for storing highly sensitive information [53]. However, most of these approaches are coupled with unbearable computation burden, which is an issue of major concern.

In this paper, a Lightweight Privacy Preserving Data Aggregation Scheme Based on Elliptic Curve for Smart Grid Communications is proposed, with the following main contribution are:

- The proposed scheme design precludes certificate and TTA or TA dependency, hence ensures system overall management requirements significantly.
- The scheme uses lightweight mathematical building blocks that are bilinear pairing-free, thus resulting in reduction of transmission delay from node to node communications.

- The proposed scheme has optimal computation and communication efficiency based on the security analysis and performance evaluation, and so the scheme has comparative advantage over other variant works, by its merits.
- Most importantly the proposed scheme ascertain user anonymity when communicating over a public channel beside providing content privacy.

In this vain, our work endeavors to design and incorporate these main contributions, and performance comparison with some state-of-the-art privacy-preserving data aggregation techniques provided. Thus, the proposed work achieves better overall communication and computation efficiency to the best comparable scheme besides better satisfaction of main security requirements.

The rest of the paper is organized as follows: Sect. 2, reviews related works in data aggregation over smart grid environment and pin-points the research gap and limitations in other researches. Then we present the generic system design model, basic mathematical and cryptographic preliminaries required for understanding the proposed scheme in Sect. 3. The proposed lightweight privacy-preserving data aggregation scheme is presented in Sect. 3. Further Sect. 4 gives the analysis and evaluation of results respectively. Finally, the conclusion and suggestions for further research are presented in Sect. 5.

2   Related Works and Limitations

A variety of techniques and approaches for privacy-preserving data aggregation (PPDA) have been proposed in literature in a quest to address the challenge of secure data aggregation to be practical in SG network environment. In [43] Liu Y., et al., proposed a 3PDA data aggregation scheme for SG, however the scheme uses computationally expensive bilinear pairings in the data collection units (DCUs) and the OC which is not ideal for a system of systems comprising of myriads of communicating devices. While in [32] He D., et al., designed an efficient PPAD scheme but is based on TTP which is not also a desirable feature in a highly populated network since it bears a bottleneck for the TTP to manage the messages with efficiency. Similarly in [37] Jo H.J., et al., asserts that their construction is efficient at the expense of using bilinear computations which contradicts the claim for a practical scheme. Additionally, in [31] is it disclosed that their scheme does not provide user privacy as the identity is transmitted in plaintext hence prone to human-factor-aware data aggregation (HDA) attacks and all sorts of privacy breaches. Other researches based their construction on computationally expensive Paillier's homomorphic cryptosystem [12,46,59], which still need some improvement to be deemed practical for smart grid because the Pailler's primitives is comparative heavier although is it widely used technique [16]. Achieving acceptable level of computational as well as communication efficiency is a default requirement for any real-time based communication technology like IoT-enhanced smart grid. In the schemes [12,46,59], theirs security is anchored in the gateway as it plays a trusted role and it provides the aggregated data to the OC. The proposed scheme in [37], does not rely on trusted gateway but rather uses a group approach to sent encrypted messages. The private key is secretly held by a group of smart meters and they collude to send an encrypted message to the AMI. In order for the AMI or OC to decrypt data, it requires the selected smart meters to help in the decryption which adds on overhead and clearly this is impractical design. Although the scheme removes trust-ship, it incurs unnecessary communication overhead in the collusion process. Also the design is prone to differential attack hence can suffer from privacy breach. To achieve this the AMI collude with participating smart meter to decrypt two different messages representing the sets which differ only by a single user. At the end the AMI can deduce the user's data from the difference of the two decrypted messages. Although the scheme [65] claims to be robust in security and efficiency, we analyzed it and found it lacking to provide user anonymity as the identity is transmitted in plain-text, hence is prone to eavesdropping, and also in [60] it was found to have its properties unattributed. In 2011, Wu and Zhou [68] proposed a key exchange scheme for smart grid based on elliptic curve cryptography (ECC) which required a trusted authority (TA) and a public key infrastructure (PKI) for key management. The authors of [68] claim their scheme is resistant to replay attacks and man-in-the-middle attacks. However in [69] Xia and Wang discovered that the scheme in [68] cannot provide replay attack and man-in-the-middle attack resilience and has even vulnerable session key. In 2018, Mahmood et al., [47] proposed an authentication scheme between two communicating entities in smart grid, however in [1] it is pointed out that the scheme in [47] has weakness of lack of perfect forward secrecy. Although in [63], it was assessed that the proposed data obfuscation approach provides good data throughput, good packet delay and delivery ratio under a variety of conditions, in [15] they found it bears high communication latency due to large bandwidth requirement and also in [60] they point out that the scheme in [63] fails to explicitly state its focusing field, whether is it for customer billing applications or grid operations. Another ECC based multi-dimensional data aggregation scheme was proposed by Boudia et al. in [10], which does not require bilinear pairings hence having efficient computation overhead. However, the scheme is flawed by being TA dependent. In [6], Badra and Zeadally, proposed an ECC based privacy-preserving data aggregation scheme by utilizing homomormphic encryption and Diffie-Hellman techniques, however it bears heavy communication overhead.

Different schemes in literature have been proposed based on different approached and methodologies. Their short-falls varies widely ranging from; having high computation overhead [2, 7, 43, 46, 59, 61, 63], prone to common attacks [11, 47, 57, 68] and high demand of system computation resources due to need of additional requirements for TTP, PKI and TA management in their designs [28, 30, 32, 33].

2.1   Generic System Model

In this section, we briefly describe the proposed data aggregation scheme's network architecture, the preliminaries building blocks for the scheme and subsequently we define the security requirements for the model. The system design of our model is depicted in Fig. 1, which consists of three main entities: SMs, data aggregation point (DAP) and the utility OC in a hierarchical structure, which follows the standard smart grid architecture [23, 25]. An OC has a number of neighborhood area networks (NANs), in turns each NAN has numerous home area networks (HANs) [21, 27, 29, 30, 35, 38]. The DAP is the gateway for a particular NAN which does data aggregation and relaying of information between OC and SM. Whereas for each HAN there is a SM enabling bi-directional communication with the DAP. In this model SMs collect real-time consumption data from the HAN and sends it to OC via DAP at 15 min regular intervals [47, 49, 60]. The communication between SM and DAP is through wireless technology such as Wi-Fi, RF mesh, 6LowPAN, ZigBee, Z-wave among other wireless communication protocols [2, 12, 65]. Smart meter transmitted data includes the bill, real-time electricity report, consumer identification and regular instruction dispatches. So, the DAP acts as a gateway for the neighborhood area network and bridges the SMs and the OC by utilizing long range and high bandwidth communication technology with low latency like WiMAX or, 3G, 4G communication technologies and wired links among others [3, 18, 19, 52, 62, 64, 65]. As a gateway the DAP aggregates the collected individual SM data to leverage the computational overhead of OC in decrypting each SM's information. Similarly, communication efficiency is still a challenging issue that requires permanent solution, since there will be hundreds or thousands of smart meters in regions reporting their electricity related information almost at the same time to the OC through the DAP.

The OC being in the utility side, is deemed honest-but-curious entity and can know customer's electricity usage during a billing period of pricing and power management. This means the OC executes operations according to the scheme without launching any active attack. On the other hand, the DAP is assumed not fully trusted since it can be easily controlled by an adversary. The user or SM is usually assumed as dishonest with some extent of trust or common interest to win incentives from the OC orders. A good property needed in this architecture is to conceal individual's electricity usage to neighboring SMs and the DAPs even in an attempt of smart meters launching a collusion attack. Thus, is necessary to secure the system from all sorts of attacks such as: data privacy attacks, relationship attacks, false data injection attacks and distortion attacks. Data privacy attack occurs when some malicious smart meter node collude with the gateway or another smart meter to obtain the real-time or total power consumption data of another uncompromised smart meter during a billing session. In relationship attack the gateway attempts to deduce user behavior and habits from the relationship between electricity consumption of different reporting intervals for one specific user. While false data injection refers to attack on the integrity of the data where an adversary introduces a code that compromises the correctness of the data. In distortion attack the gateway tries to forge a user's real-time power usage in order to disturb the billing system in smart grid.

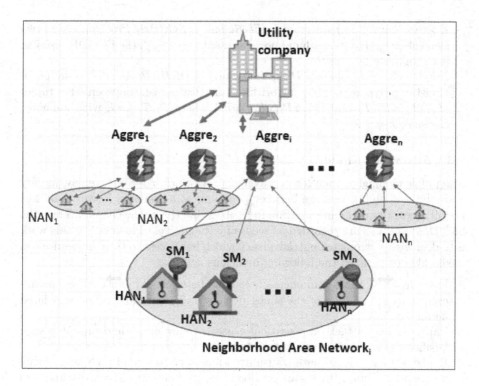

Fig. 1. Generic system model.

2.2 Preliminaries

Now, we will formalize the background knowledge of the building blocks for the proposed scheme. ECC is a public key cryptosystem based on elliptic curve theory and has an advantage for being a structure for faster and more efficient cryptosystems with robust security. ECC cryptosystems have low computational requirement hence making it as viable mechanism for securing IoT based systems with numerous resource constrained devices and real-time operations like in SG system [57,66].

- *Elliptic curve*: Given a prime number q, the equation $y^3 = x^2 + ax + b\,mod\,p$ defines an elliptic curve over a prime field $E(F_p)$, where $p > 3, a, b \in F_q$ and satisfies $\triangle = 4a^3 + 27b^2 \neq 0\ mod\,p$. The points on F_p together with the point at infinity $\mathcal{O}$ form an additive cyclic group G. Let P be the generator point of order n, the scalar multiple operation is defined as, $nP = P + P + \cdots + P$, for n times addition, where $n \in Z_q^*$, is a positive integer. So, there are a number of intractable problems in an elliptic curve group, G, of order n, suitable for cryptographic purposes as there is no polynomial time algorithm to solve them efficiently by brute-force within probabilistic polynomial time.
- *Elliptic Discrete Logarithm (ECDL) Problem*: Given an element $Q \in G$, the ECDL problem is to extract an element $x \in Z_q^*$, such that $Q = xP$.

- *Elliptic Curve Computational Diffie-Hellman (ECCDH) Problem*: Given two elements $xP, yP \in G$, with unknown elements $x, y \in Z_q^*$, the ECCDH problem is to compute $Q = xyP$.
- *Elliptic Curve Decisional Diffie-Hellman (ECDDH) Problem*: No any probabilistic polynomial time algorithm can distinguish between the tuples (P_1, xP_1, yP_1, T) and (P_1, xP_1, yP_1, xyP_1) where $P_1, T \in G$, with unknown elements $x, y \in Z_q^*$.

2.3 Adversary Model

The public channel is open for an adversary, $\mathcal{A}$, which can forge, replay, modify and intercept plying message between communicating parties. However, $\mathcal{A}$, has no full access to private information from observing the public channel. Thus, the SM, DAP and OC are regarded as secure by themselves. The focus in this work is to deal with a strong enough adversary which has access to the communication media able to perform the following malicious actions:

- Eavesdropping the communication channel between SM and DAP communications to get an idea of the smart devices usage data and other associated details.
- Impersonation attack on a particular user's smart meter and probably send falsified data on behalf of the targeted user.
- Replay attack of legitimate transmitted messages to resend them after being intercepted. This attack can overload the authentication process and can result into transmission delay, denial of service (DoS) attack and communication bandwidth.
- Man-in-the-middle attack where by an adversary can actively eavesdrop on legitimate user's communications and relay modified messages between legitimate users making them believe they are communicating with intended counterpart.

2.4 Security Requirements

There is need to satisfy basic security requirements for the proposed scheme to ascertain the claimed security of the transmitted electricity reports from the consumer to the data aggregation points over the public channel as well as regulation and control commands originating from operation center to the consumer. Obviously, the data aggregation scheme faces all kinds of attacks from an adversary in between SM and DAP. The proposed scheme, achieves these attributes without relying on TTP or certificate issuance to facilitate the authentication process. Thus, our scheme design ensures conformity of the following prescribed requirements.

- *Authentication*: The DAP has to validate the true identity of the smart meter to make sure the data it receives really comes from the smart meter. Thus, the communicating entities should ascertain that they are communicating with the intended counterpart. This measure checks possible malicious acts such as message forgery, impersonation and masquerading attacks.

- *Data Confidentiality*: The mechanism must avoid any leakage of an individual's electricity usage data that could pose privacy breach. So, it is necessary to ascertain that no-one either internal or external attacker, extracts any individual's electricity usage data. So, confidentiality of user's electricity consumption data is very necessary since its leakage can reveal user's habit or identity which eventually exposes the user to attacks.
- *Data Integrity*: This mechanism ensures consistency and trustworthiness of the transmitted data, so that data is not altered nor modified by unauthorized party while in transit or elsewhere. This feature is of significantly importance in smart grid so that the data aggregation process should uphold integrity and message modification or forgery, and should there be any attempt for such attacks, should be detected.
- *Consumer Privacy and Anonymity*: The actual identity of a consumer in a community should not be known by any malicious party eavesdropping on the communications between consumer and OC. Thus, even if two instances of consumption data reports are eavesdropped the adversary should not distinguish if the two consumption reporting data are from the same user or not. Thus, a scheme zshould uphold user anonymity during the message flow of the concerned parties.
- *Attack Resilience*: Due to communication over a public channel, the data aggregation scheme must ensure security to withstand common attacks such as: impersonation attack, replay attack, modification attack and man-in-the-middle-attack [22,41].

In regard to the discussed system model and security requirements, our main goal is to design a secure and efficient scheme for privacy-preserving data aggregation for smart grid AMI communications.

3 Proposed Scheme

We will present the framework of the proposed Lightweight Privacy-Preserving Data Aggregation (LPPDA) Scheme Based on Elliptic Curve Cryptography for Smart Grid Communications. The notation description of the symbols used in the proposed scheme is outlined in Table 1. Our construction suggests the variant construction of an El Gamal encryptosystem and an additive homomorphic encryption algorithm applied over elliptic curve field whose properties are:

(a) In order to encrypt a message m into a ciphertext C using an El Gamal approach, the sender, uses the public key of a receiver $pk = xP$, generates a random number $r \in Z_q^*$, with it computes $C_a = rP$ and $C_b = (pk)r + mP$. Thus an encryption process proceeds as:

$$E_{pk}(m) = (C_a, C_b) = (rP, r(pk) + mP) = C$$

Table 1. Notations used in our scheme

Symbols	Meanings of symbols in the scheme
p, q	Two large primes
E	Is the chosen elliptic curve, $y^3 = x^2 + ax + b \bmod p$ where $a, b \in Z_q^*$
$E(F_p)$	Is the prime field of an elliptic curve E order p
P	Is the generator of $E(F_p)$ with large prime order q
G	A cyclic group generated by a point P on a non-singular elliptic curve E
ID_s	Identity of smart meter user, SM_i
t_s, t_d	Timestamps for SM and DAP
e_i	Electricity consumption generated by a smart meter at t_s
δ	The time lapse for an interval of time from t_s to t_d
pk, sk	Public key and private key respectively
$E_{pk}(.)$	Encryption algorithm by using a public key pk
$D_{sk}(.)$	Decryption algorithm by using a private key sk
X_s, x_s	Public key and private key of smart meter user respectively
X_d, x_d	Public key and private key of gateway respectively
X_α, x_α	Public key and private key of utility company
H_1, H_2	Hash function: H_1, $H_2 : \{0,1\}^* \rightarrow Z_q^*$
$\oplus$	Exclusive-OR operation (XOR)
$\|$	Concatenation

(b) So to decrypt a ciphertext C, the receiver uses its private key $sk = x$, and carry out the following operation.

$$D_{sk}(C) = D_{sk}(E_{pk}(m)) = (r(pk) + mP) - (sk)(rP)$$
$$= (r(xP) + mP) - x(rP)$$
$$= mP$$

After which the message m can be retrieved by using the Pollards lambda method.

(c) For additive homomorphic property, we suppose there are two messages encryption instances m_1 and m_2 transformed into two respective ciphertext instances C_1 and C_2 as follows.

$$E_{pk}(m_1) + E_{pk}(m_2) = (r_1 P, r_1(pk) + m_1 P) + (r_2 P, r_2(pk) + m_2 P)$$
$$= ((r_1 P + r_2 P), ((r_1 pk + m_1 P) + (r_2 pk + m_2 P))$$
$$= ((r_1 + r_2)P, (r_1 pk + r_2 pk) + (m_1 P + m_2 P))$$
$$= ((r_1 + r_2)P, (r_1 + r_2)pk + (m_1 + m_2)P)$$
$$= E_{pk}(m_1 + m_2)$$
$$= (C_1 + C_2)$$

(d) Scalar multiplication property.

$$E_{pk}(cx) = \underbrace{E_{pk}(x) + E_{pk}(x) + \cdots + E_{pk}(x)}_{c\text{-times}}$$

$$= \sum_{i=1}^{c} E_{pk}(x)$$

where $+$ is the additive homomorphic encryption operation and c is a constant for scalar multiplication.

The construction of the scheme consists of the following five algorithms, namely System Initialization, Key Generation, Smart Meter Data Reporting, Data Aggregation and Data Recovery as explained below.

(a) **System Initialization**: OC runs a system initialization algorithm with 1^k as a security parameter and outputs a cyclic group G of prime order q, with $P \in G$ as its generator, an elliptic curve $E : y^2 = x^3 + ax + b \; modp$, where $a, b \in F_p$, for F_p a prime field of order p. The OC then chooses P from the elliptic curve E, by using P generates a group G of order q. Later OC chooses $x_\alpha \in Z_q^*$ as its master secret key (private key) and $X_\alpha = x_\alpha P$ as its public key. OC selects secure hash functions: $H_1 : \{0,1\}^* \rightarrow Z_q^*$, $H_2 : \{0,1\}^* \rightarrow Z_q^*$. After initialization the following public parameters for system management are published, $params = \{P, p, q, E, F_p, G, X_\alpha, H_1, H_2\}$.

(b) **Key Generation**: After system parameter initialization each smart meter is issued with a private key x_s whose corresponding public key is, $X_s = x_s P$. Similarly the neighborhood or residential area gateway, DAP is securely issued with a pair of public and private key as, X_d and x_d respectively, where $X_d = x_d P$ and $x_d \in Z_q^*$.

(c) **Smart Meter Data Reporting**: The smart meter uses the public keys of the DAP and OC to send a cipher-text for smart metering data report for a particular period of time. For management purposes, the electricity reports from SMs to OC are transmitted in 10 - 15 min intervals. Let e_i represents an individual user's electricity consumption report in the specified time interval for $i = 1, 2, \cdots, n$. The SM deployed at household is in charge of all home appliances, and it collects the usage data, and then encrypts it before transmission to the DAP. Before SM sends the data, e_i to the receiver, it is necessary to map the message e_i to a point on the elliptic curve using a homomorphic mapping as $m_i = e_i G$. Then later, the SM carries out data encryption procedure by using the public keys of DAP and OC which are, x_d, X_α respectively as follows:

  • Step 1: Each smart meter generates random numbers, $r_d, r_\alpha \in Z_q^*$, and then computes $C_1 = r_d P$, $C_2 = r_\alpha P$, $C_3 = r_\alpha X_\alpha \oplus ID_s$ then encrypts the data as, $C_i = m_i + ID_s + r_\alpha X_\alpha + r_d X_d$. Furthermore, the SM computes the authentication and integrity check component $\sigma_1 = H_1(C_i||C_1||X_s||t_s)x_s$, by using its own private key as a signature and public with its timestamp t_s

- Step 2: Then the smart meter sends $M_1 = \{C_1, C_2, C_3, C_i, X_s, t_s, \sigma_1\}$ to the DAP of its residential area network. Thus C_i is the actual cipher-text of the reporting data.

Furthermore, its worth to take note that, C_1, C_2 and C_3 can be pre-computed to expedite the smart meter data reporting process.

(d) **DAP Data Aggregation**: Upon receipt of the message M_1 from SM, the gateway (DAP) has to perform aggregation on the encrypted data and partially decrypt the message to leverage the OC of some computational overhead by using its private key. DAP proceeds as follows:

- step 1: Selects the timestamps t_d, and checks the validity by computing $|t_d - t_s| < \delta$ otherwise it aborts the session, where δ is the acceptable threshold of time lapse.
- step 2: Checks both the source and message authenticity and validity of the received message by verifying that $\sigma_1.P = H_1(C_i||C_1||X_s||t_s)X_s$ and it proceeds only if the computation holds
- Step 3: First computes, $Y_d = x_d C_1$ and then DAP carries out data aggregation by partial decryption of the message from SM to OC as follows:

$$C_T^{agg} = \sum_{i=1}^{n}(C_i - Y_d)$$
$$= \sum_{i=1}^{n}(m_i + ID_s + r_\alpha X_\alpha)$$

which is the result of additive homomorphic operation on an encrypted data

- step 4: Then DAP computes a signature of the partially decrypted cipher-text, including both its private key and public key in the computation , $\sigma_2 = H_2(C_T^{agg}||C_2||C_3||X_d||t_d)x_d$.
- step 5: Now DAP forwards the partially decrypted message $M_2 = \{C_2, C_3, C_T^{agg}, X_d, t_d, \sigma_2\}$ to the OC.

(e) **Data Recovery**: Upon receipt of the partially decrypted message M_2 from DAP, the OC carries the following steps in the process of decrypting.

- step 1: Selects the timestamp t_α, and checks if $|t_\alpha - t_d| < \delta$ holds and then proceeds, otherwise it quits the process.
- step 2: Furthermore the OC checks the integrity of the partially decrypted ciphertext from the DAP by verifying, $\sigma_2.P = H_2(C_T^{agg}||C_2||C_3||X_d||t_d)X_d$.
- step 3: Afterwards, OC carries out user identification extraction by computing:

$$ID_s = C_3 \oplus C_2.x_\alpha$$

- step 4: Finally, the OC is able to securely extract the total electricity consumption reporting data for each user by carrying out the computation:

$$Cons_{Total} = C_T^{agg} - \sum_{i=1}^{n}(ID_s + x_\alpha C_2)$$

$$= \sum_{i=1}^{n} m_i + \sum_{i=1}^{n} ID_s + r_\alpha X_\alpha - \sum_{i=1}^{n} (ID_s + x_\alpha C_2)$$

$$= \sum_{i=1}^{n} (m_i + ID_s + r_\alpha X_\alpha) - \sum_{i=1}^{n} (ID_s + x_\alpha r_\alpha P)$$

$$= \sum_{i=1}^{n} m_i$$

It should be noticed that, if any checking in the scheme's steps fails to hold then the scheme is immediately aborted. A summary of message flow for the scheme between concerned entities is depicted in Table 2.

Now we can look at the correctness of the main computations of DAP and OC to verify he consistence of the messages.

DAP Computation Correctness:

$$Y_d = x_d C_1$$
$$= x_d r_d P$$
$$= r_d x_d P$$
$$= r_d X_d$$

The DAP computes partial decryption:

$$C_T^{agg} = \sum_{i=1}^{n} (C_i - Y_d)$$

$$= \sum_{i=1}^{n} (m_i + ID_s + r_\alpha X_\alpha + r_d X_d + k_i - x_d C_1)$$

$$= \sum_{i=1}^{n} (m_i + ID_s + r_\alpha X_\alpha + r_d X_d + k_i - x_d r_d P)$$

$$= \sum_{i=1}^{n} (m_i + ID_s + r_\alpha X_\alpha + r_d X_d + k_i - r_d x_d P)$$

$$= \sum_{i=1}^{n} (m_i + ID_s + r_\alpha X_\alpha + k_i)$$

$$= \sum_{i=1}^{n} (m_i + ID_s + r_\alpha X_\alpha) + \sum_{i=1}^{n} k_i$$

$$= \sum_{i=1}^{n} (m_i + ID_s + r_\alpha X_\alpha)$$

OC Computation Correctness:
Extraction of ID_s:

$$ID_s = C_3 \oplus C_2 x_\alpha$$

$$= (r_\alpha X_\alpha \oplus ID_s) \oplus (r_\alpha P)x_\alpha$$
$$= (r_\alpha X_\alpha \oplus ID_s) \oplus (r_\alpha X_\alpha)$$
$$= r_\alpha X_\alpha \oplus ID_s \oplus r_\alpha X_\alpha$$
$$= ID_s \oplus r_\alpha X_\alpha \oplus r_\alpha X_\alpha$$

Electricity data extraction:

$$Cons_{Total} = C_T^{agg} - \sum_{i=1}^{n}(ID_s + x_\alpha C_2)$$
$$= \sum_{i=1}^{n}(m_i + ID_s + r_\alpha X_\alpha) - \sum_{i=1}^{n}(ID_s + x_\alpha C_2)$$
$$= \sum_{i=1}^{n}(m_i + ID_s + r_\alpha X_\alpha) - \sum_{i=1}^{n}(ID_s + x_\alpha r_\alpha P)$$
$$= \sum_{i=1}^{n}m_i + \sum_{i=1}^{n}(ID_s + r_\alpha X_\alpha) - \sum_{i=1}^{n}(ID_s + X_\alpha r_\alpha)$$
$$= \sum_{i=1}^{n}m_i + \sum_{i=1}^{n}(ID_s + r_\alpha X_\alpha) - \sum_{i=1}^{n}(ID_s + X_\alpha r_\alpha)$$
$$= \sum_{i=1}^{n}m_i$$

The actual total consumption data $\sum_{i=1}^{n}e_i$ is extracted from $\sum_{i=1}^{n}m_iG$ by applying the Pollard lombda operation since $e_i = m_iG$.

Thus, this shows that the computations are consistently correct as the entities in the scheme carry out them.

4 Security Analysis and Performance Evaluation

We will first give formal security and privacy proofs by random oracle model of the proposed electricity power consumption aggregation scheme and then conduct a performance evaluation in terms of computational overhead and communication overhead to demonstrate the feasibility of the proposed scheme's merits.

4.1 Security Requirements Analysis

Here we will analyze the satisfaction of security requirements of the proposed scheme and also compare it with other related works.

1. **Authentication**: The messages plying between SM and DAP as well as the ones between DAP and OC are intrinsically authenticated by either party to assure the communication is with the rightful or intended entity. The

Table 2. LPPDA scheme message flow.

Smart meter (SM)	Data Aggregator (DAP)	Operation Center (OC)
SM Computes:		
$C_1 = r_d P$, s.t $r_d \in Z_q^*$		
$C_2 = r_\alpha P$, s.t $r_\alpha \in Z_q^*$		
$C_3 = r_\alpha X_\alpha \oplus ID_s$		
$C_i = m_i + ID_s + r_\alpha X_\alpha + r_d X_d + k_i$		
$\sigma_1 = H_1(C_i \| C_1 \| X_s \| t_s) x_s$		
$\xrightarrow{\quad M_1 = \{C_1, C_2, C_3, C_i, t_s, X_s, \sigma_1\} \quad}$		
	DAP Data Aggregation	
	Checks if:	
	$\|t_d - t_s\| < \delta$	
	$\sigma_1 . P = H_1(C_i \| C_1 \| X_s \| t_s) X_s$	
	Then DAP computes:	
	$Y_d = x_d C_1$	
	$C_T^{agg} = \sum_{i=1}^n (C_i - Y_d)$	
	$\sigma_2 = H_2(C_T^{agg} \| C_2 \| C_3 \| X_d \| t_d) x_d$	
	$\xrightarrow{\quad M_2 = \{C_2, C_3, C_T^{agg}, X_d, t_d, \sigma_2\} \quad}$	
		OC Data Recovery
		Checks if:
		$\|t_\alpha - t_d\| < \delta$
		$\sigma_2 . P = H_2(C_T^{agg} \| C_2 \| C_3 \| X_d \| t_d) X_d$
		Then OC computes:
		$ID_s = C_3 \oplus C_2 . x_\alpha$
		$Cons = C_T^{agg} - \sum_{i=1}^n (ID_s + x_\alpha C_2)$

message, $\{C_1, C_2, C_3, C_i, X_s, t_s, \sigma_1\}$, is authenticated by DAP by checking that $\sigma_1.P = H_1(C_i \| C_1 \| X_s \| t_s) X_s$ in the message M_1 against the timestamp t_s. This checking additionally affirms the sender as legitimate since it works as a digital signature as σ_1 is generated by SM's private key and verified with its public key. Similarly, the receiver is authenticated before carrying out partial decryption by ensuring that it is able to calculate $Y_d = x_d C_1$, which is used in the partial decryption. The message is designed such that only the intended DAP, is the one able to compute $Y_d = x_d C_1$, since the computation requires a private key of DAP. Hence this entails the partially decrypted data C_T^{agg} sent to OC is an authenticated one. In turn upon extraction of user ID_s, C_T^{agg} is further used to calculate the total consumption report, which ensures authentication of the smart meter user, ID_s, to OC. Consequently the message itself and the source authentication is satisfied.

2. **Data Confidentiality**: In order to obtain the electricity consumption reporting data the OC must compute $Cons_{Total} = C_T^{agg} - \sum_{i=1}^n ID_s (x_\alpha C_2)$ of which is infeasible to be calculated by any malicious party without the specific knowledge of the private key x_α and the hidden identity ID_s. An attacker will have to solve an intractable problem of ECCDH to obtain x_α from the public key $X_\alpha = x_\alpha P$ as well as extracting ID_s from $C_3 = r_\alpha X_\alpha \oplus ID_s$, which is impossible. Therefore, the proposed scheme does meet the data confidentiality requirement.

3. **Data Integrity**: In the proposed scheme the ciphertext integrity is ensured by inclusion of verifiable signatures and freshness checking values. In the ciphertext M_1, σ_1 is used to check the integrity of the sent message to DAP

by verifying whether $\sigma_1.P = H_1(C_i||C_1||X_s||t_s)X_s$ holds. This subsequently checks the integrity of the sent message as well as the source . Likewise σ_2 upholds the integrity of the ciphertext M_2 from DAP to OC and if the verification of $\sigma_2.P = H_2(C_T^{agg}||C_2||C_3||X_d||t_d)X_d$ fails the session will be aborted. Since no attacker can generate a valid σ_1 associated with the ciphertext C_i as it is infeasible to calculate the components r_d, r_α, ID_s and m_i from the publicly accessible message M_1. Similarly, σ_2 cannot be forged to fake the authenticity of the message M_2, as it is impossible for an attacker to fabricate C_T^{agg} without knowledge of DAP's private key x_d. Thus, the proposed scheme provides message integrity.

4. **Consumer Privacy and Anonymity**: In the proposed scheme an attacker has no access to any consumer related information from the plying messages from SM to OC. The user related information in $C_3 = r_\alpha X_\alpha \oplus ID_s$ and $C_i = m_i + ID_s + r_\alpha X_\alpha + r_d X_d$ from SM to DAP is transmitted in concealed form and cannot be obtained by an attacker before solving an intractable ECCDH problem to obtain the ID_s from $C_3 = r_\alpha X_\alpha \oplus ID_s$. This is well known hard problem for an attacker to resolve, hence the proposed scheme LPPDA provides consumer privacy and anonymity befitting the wireless communication between SM and DAP, where eavesdropping can easily be done in the public channel.

5. **Attack Resilience**: The proposed LPPDA scheme has the merits to resist against well known attacks such as: replay attack, impersonation attack and man-in-the-middle attack.
   - *Replay attack*: User electricity data report from SM to OC for a particular time slot $i = 1, 2, \cdots, n$ is hashed in $\sigma_1 = H_1(C_i||C_1||X_s||t_s)x_s$ which comprises of fresh random numbers r_d and r_α for each session run. Similarly, OC verifies the freshness of M_2 by checking that $\sigma_2 = H_2(C_T^{agg}||C_2||C_3||X_s||t_d)x_d$ holds. Thus, the timestamp t_s and t_d checks against any replay attempts by an attacker on the messages M_1 and M_2 respectively. Therefore by this procedure, LPPDA could resist replay attack.
   - *Impersonation attack*: No attacker can produce the ciphertext $C_i = m_i + ID_s + r_\alpha X_\alpha + r_d X_d$ associated with the identity ID_s without knowledge of either random number r_d or the private key, x_d. Thus, an attacker has no idea of the user who is to be impersonated on. By this, LPPDA is able to resist any impersonation attack.
   - *Man-in-the-middle attack*: From the ciphertext M_2 obtained by OC originating from SM, only the OC could extract the identity ID_s that authenticates SM to OC in the process $ID_s = C_3 \oplus C_2.x_\alpha$. Furthermore, the integrity check components, $\sigma_1 = H_1(C_i||C_1||X_s||t_s)x_s$ and $\sigma_2 = H_2(C_T^{agg}||C_2||C_3||X_d||t_s)x_d$ are generated with sender's private key to be verified by its corresponding public key, meaning that no attacker can formulate a verifiable ciphertext impersonating ID_s to DAP and OC, because of lack of private keys of the victims. Therefore an attacker in between SM and DAP cannot generate valid C_i and σ_1 that can be verified. Similarly the messages from DAP to OC are secure from an attacker

in between as C_T^{agg} cannot be forged for a targeted identity ID_s as it is verified by σ_2.

Furthermore, the merits of the proposed LPPDA scheme are compared against other related schemes [44, 46, 48, 61, 65] with respect to security features satisfied, as shown in the Table 3. In the table the ✓ symbol shows that a particular security feature is satisfied while the ✗ symbol shows that the security feature is not satisfied. For easy representation in the table the following features: confidentiality, authentication, integrity, anonymity, replay attack, impersonation attack, internal attack and man-in-the-middle attack are denoted as, F1, F2, F3, F4, F5, F6, F7, F8 respectively. So clearly, it is evident from the Table 3, that LPPDA scheme has merits on satisfaction of security requirements over related works.

Table 3. Security comparison

Security features comparison								
Scheme	F1	F2	F3	F4	F5	F6	F7	F8
[44]	✓	✗	✗	✗	✓	✓	✗	✗
[46]	✓	✓	✓	✗	✓	✓	✗	✓
[48]	✓	✓	✓	✗	✓	✓	✓	✓
[65]	✓	✓	✓	✗	✓	✓	✓	✓
[61]	✓	✓	✓	✗	✓	✓	✗	✗
LPPDA	✓	✓	✓	✓	✓	✓	✓	✓

4.2 Performance Evaluation

In this section, performance analysis is carried out in comparison with relevant related schemes [44, 46, 48, 61, 65] based on computational cost required for SM, DAP and OC as well as the communication cost analysis of the channels SM to DAP and DAP to OC respectively are presented.

4.3 Computation Cost

The computational times variables used in LPPDA, for carrying out specific cryptographic operations are adapted from [48] which were simulated on MIRACL Crypto SDK, which is a multi-precision integer, rational arithmetic C/C++ library, [58] run on a 2.53 GHz i5 CPU, 4 GB RAM on a 64 bit windows 10 operating system. The experimentation used a 160 bit key length for security parameters chosen from G over F_p. The data of the average quantified running times is depicted in given Table 4, which was obtained after taking the averages of 1000 runs in the simulation.

Table 4. Estimated running times for different operations in milliseconds (ms) averaged after 1000 runs

Notations	Description of operation	Execution time
T_{sm-ecc}	Scalar multiplication in ECC	0.38
T_{DL}	Solving DL operetion in $\bmod p$	0.64
T_{mtp}	Map to a point hash function	3.58
T_{n^2}	Exponentiation in Z_{n^2}	2.02
T_p	Bilinear paring	10.31
T_{p-D}	Paillier public key decryption	11.82
T_{p-E}	Paillier public key encryption	9.89
T_{exp-p}	Exponentiation in p	0.13
T_m	Scalar multiplication in bilinear paring	1.42
T_n	Exponentiation in Z_n	0.58

In this regard the computation cost comparison will be done based on the quantification weights in Table 4, averaged after 1000 experiment runs in order to estimate time complexities for different operations. In this evaluation, lightweight operations like hash functions, hash chain, concatenation, point addition and XORing are disregarded, since they have negligible computation overload. So, our focus will be on heavier computation operations only such as: map-to-point hash function, bilinear parings, paillier public key encryption and paillier public key decryption operations among others as portrayed in the Table 5.

Table 5. Computed average running times of schemes for different operations in milliseconds

Scheme	SM	DAP	OC	Total time
[44]	$1T_m + (n+1)T_{n^2} + 1T_{mtp}$ $= 2.02n + 7.02ms$	$(w+1)T_p + 1T_m + (w+1)T_{mtp}$ $= 13.89w + 15.70ms$	$2T_p + 1T_{mtp}$ $= 36.04ms$	$13.89w + 2.02n + 58.74ms$
[46]	$3T_{exp-p} + 3T_m$ $= 4.65ms$	$(3w+1)T_{exp-p} + 3T_m$ $= 0.39w + 4.39ms$	$4T_{exp-p} + 3T_m$ $= 4.78ms$	$0.39w + 13.82ms$
[48]	$6T_{sm-ecc}$ $= 2.28ms$	$(2w+2)T_{sm-ecc}$ $= 0.76w + 0.76ms$	$4T_{sm-ecc} + 1T_{DL}$ $= 2.16ms$	$0.76w + 5.2ms$
[65]	$5T_{sm-ecc}$ $= 1.9ms$	$2T_p + (w+1)T_{sm-ecc}$ $= 0.38w + 21ms$	$1T_p + (2z+1)T_{sm-ecc} + 1T_{mtp}$ $= 4.78z + 14.26ms$	$= 0.38w + 4.78z + 37.16ms$
[61]	$3T_{exp-p} + 3T_m$ $= 4.65ms$	$(3w+1)T_{exp-p} + 3T_m$ $= 0.39w + 4.39ms$	$4T_{exp-p} + 3T_m$ $= 4.78ms$	$0.39w + 13.82ms$
LPPDA	$6T_{sm-ecc}$ $= 2.28ms$	wT_{sm-ecc} $= (1.14w)ms$	$(z+3)T_{sm-ecc}$ $= (0.76z)ms$	$= 0.76w + 0.38z + 3.68ms$

The computational cost is categorized in three levels according to the entity carrying out the operation which are the smart meters, data aggregation points and the operations center for the sake of clarity and fairness in the evaluation. Thus, we will evaluate the computational cost of the SM, DAP and OC individually before calculating the total computation incurred in the schemes [44, 46, 48, 61, 65] and the summary of the comparison is done in Table 5.

Firstly, we calculate computational cost required for a SM in different schemes. The computational cost required for SM in [44] is $(n + 1)$ exponentiation operations in Z_{n^2}, one map-to-point hash operation and one scalar multiplication in bilinear pairing. So the amount of the computation cost for a SM is $(n+1)T_{n^2} + 1T_m + 1T_{mtp} = 2.02 + 7n.02ms$. In schemes [46] and [61], there are three exponentiation operations in G_1 and three scalar multiplication in bilinear pairing. So the amount of computation needed for SM is $3T_{exp-p} + 3T_m = 4.65ms$. While in [48], SM needs six scalar multiplication which amounts to $6T_{sm-ecc} = 2.28ms$ and in [65] five scalar multiplication operations are needed with an overhead of $5T_{sm-ecc} = 1.9ms$. On the other hand in LPPDA, SM requires six scalar multiplication with the computational cost of $6T_{sm-ecc} = 2.28ms$. However, although [65] has the same SM computational cost as in the proposed scheme, in LPPDA scheme the computation of which, C_1, C_2 and C_3 can be pre-computated prior to the data reporting time and this further reduces the computational requirement. Thus, our design would require $3T_{sm-ecc} = 1.14ms$ for real-time computations, therefore it does not overload the SM computation overhead during the run time, besides it ensures provision of user anonymity, unlike in the other schemes.

Secondly, the computation cost for DAP in these schemes is such that in [44] there are $w + 1$ bilinear pairing operations where w is the numbers of smart meters in a particular neighborhood, one scalar multiplication in bilinear pairing and $w + 1$ map-to-point hash operations. Consequently, the DAP requires $(w+1)T_p + 1T_m + (w+1)T_{mtp} = 13.89w + 15.7ms$ computation cost. Whereas in [46] and [61], the schemes need $3w + 1$ exponentiation operations in G_1 and three scalar multiplication operations in bilinear pairing and DAP's computation cost is $(3w+1)T_{exp-p}+3T_m = 0.39w+4.39ms$. In scheme [48], the DAP requires $(2w+2)$ scalar multiplication operations with a computation cost overhead of $(2w+2)T_{sm-ecc} = 0.76w + 0.76ms$. Whereas in [65], two bilinear pairing operations and $(w + 1)$ scalar multiplication are needed so the computation cost overhead for DAP is $2T_p + (w+1)T_{sm-ecc} = 0.38w + 21ms$. On the other hand the DAP in the proposed LPPDA, requires $3w$ scalar multiplication operations and one exponentiation operation, thus the computation cost for DAP is $3wT_{sm-ecc} = (1.14w)ms$.

Thirdly, we analyze the computation cost required for OC in each scheme and we assume that there are z, DAPs in the wide area network where OC is incharge. In Lu et' al [44] scheme, OC requires to two bilinear pairing operations, one paillier public key decryption operation and one map-to-point hash operation. The computation cost required in this case is $2T_p + 1T_{p-D} + 1T_{mtp} = 36.04$. Whereas in [46] and [61], the OC requires four exponentiation operations in G_1, three scalar multiplication operations in bilinear pairings, so the computation cost overhead is $4T_{exp-p} + 3T_m = 4.78ms$. In Ming et al. [48], on the other hand, OC requires four scalar multiplication operations and DL operation $mod\ p$, with the computational cost of $4T_{sm-ecc} + 1T_{DL} = 2.16ms$. In [65], the OC needs one bilinear pairing operation, $(2z + 1)$ scalar multiplication operation and one map-to-point hash operation, resulting into the computation cost of $1T_p + (2z+1)T_{sm-ecc} + 1T_{mtp} = 4.78z + 14.26ms$. While in the proposed

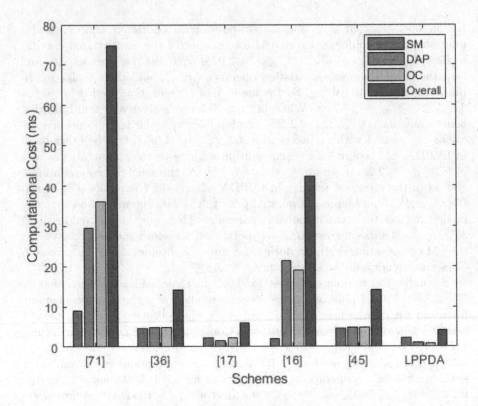

Fig. 2. Computation cost for the schemes.

LPPDA, the OC requires $2zT_{sm-ecc}$ scalar multiplication operations yielding to computation cost of $2zT_{sm-ecc} = 0.76zms$.

Thus, with reference to the computation loads of each entity reflected in Table 5, where w stands for the number of smart meters reporting to DAP and z stands for number of DAPs reporting to OC. The proposed LPPDA scheme has overall lower computation cost as depicted in Fig. 2, with both w and z equated to one for simplicity, even though [48] and [65] have a slightest edge for lower SM overhead. The computation results considers the incurred overhead per individual entity, that is SM, DAP and OC separately. The actual run time computation cost for SM is much lower to the tune of $1.14ms$ upon excluding pre-computated operations unlike the $2.28ms$ shown in the Fig. 2, of which is still lower than comparable schemes hence affirming the efficiency of the proposed LPPDA scheme.

4.4   Communication Cost

Now we will evaluate the communication cost of the proposed LPPDA scheme in relation to the schemes [44, 46, 48, 61, 65], however ECC based schemes are generally more efficient and saves more bandwidth since with reduced short length security parameter with high security achievement. Different mathematical structures have different lengths for the security parameters. The elements in G_1, G_T, G, Z_q^*, Z_n and Z_{n^2} respectively, have the lengths, 512 bits, 1024 bits, 160 bits, 160 bits, 1024 bits and 2048 bits. The length of a hash function is 160 bits whilst that for an identity and timestamp is 32 bits. The communication cost analysis between SM and DAP is given as follows. SM sends the message $\{C_i, \sigma_i, RA, U_i, TS\}$ to the DAP in [46], such that $C_i \in Z_{n^2}$, $\sigma_i \in G_1$ whereby RA, U_i and TS are all 32 bit long each. SM to DAP communication cost is therefore, $|C_i + \sigma_i + RA + U_i + TS| = 2048 + 512 + 32 + 32 + 32 = 2659$ bits. Whereas in scheme [44], the SM sends the message C_i of length $|C_i| = 1024$ bits. While in [48] et 'al, the message $\{C_{1,i}, C_{2,i}, ID_i, L_i, v_i, T\}$ is sent from SM to DAP with the overall communication load of $|C_{1,i} + C_{2,i} + ID_i + L_i + v_i + T| = 160 + 160 + 32 + 160 + 160 + 32 = 704$, where $C_{1,i}, C_{2,i}, L_i \in G$, $v_i \in Z_q^*$ and further, ID_i and T are both 32 bit identity and timestamp respectively. On the other hand, in the scheme [65], SM sends the message $R_{it}||S_{it}||t||ID_{U_i}||\sigma_{it}$ to corresponding DAP. By considering the same conditions for [65] elements in the group G has length of 160 bits. Thus, the communication bandwidth required for [65] is, $|R_{it} + S_{it} + t + ID_{U_i} + \sigma_{it}| = 160 + 160 + 32 + 32 + 160 = 544$ bits. In the scheme [61], SM sends the message $\{C_i, H_i\}$ to DAP with $C_i \in G_T$ and H_i a one way hash function. The computation cost requirement is therefore, $|C_i + H_i| = 1024 + 160 = 1184$ bits. On the on other hand, in the proposed LPPDA, SM sends the message $M_1 = \{C_1, C_2, C_3, C_i, X_s, t_s, \sigma_1\}$ to DAP all from the group G. So the required communication bandwidth is $|C_1 + C_2 + C_3 + C_i + X_s + t_s + \sigma_1| = 160 + 160 + 160 + 160 + 160 + 32 + 160 = 992$.

Lastly, the communication cost between DAP and OC in the concerned schemed is analyzed as follows. DAP sends the message $\{C, \sigma_g, RA, GW, TS\}$ to OC in [44], where $C \in Z_{n^2}$. $\sigma_g \in G_1$, and further, RA and TS are both 32 bits elements. Thus, the communication cost is $|C + \sigma_g + RA + GW + TS| = 2048 + 512 + 32 + 32 + 32 = 2659$ bits. The DAP in [46] sends C as the message to OC where $C \in G_T$, so the communication cost is $|C| = 1024$ bits. On the other hand, DAP sends the message $\{C_1, C_2, ID_{GW}, L_{GW}, v_{GW}, T\}$ to OC in [48], with $C_1, C_2, L_{GW} \in G$, $v_{GW} \in Z_q^*$ and further, ID_{GW} and T are both 32 bits long elements. Hence the communication cost amounts to $|C_1 + C_2 + ID_{GW} + L_{GW} + v_{GW} + T| = 160 + 160 + 32 + 160 + 160 + 32 = 704$ bits. In [65], the DAP sends the message $R_t||S_t||t||ID_{AG_j}||\sigma_{AG_j,t}$ to OC, so the communication cost is $|R_t + S_t + t + ID_{AG_j} + \sigma_{AG_j,t}| = 160 + 160 + 32 + 32 + 1024 = 1408$ bits. While in Tahir et al. [61], DAP sends the message, $\{C, H\}$ to OC with $C \in G_T$ and H as a 160 bits one-way hansh function, therefore yielding the communication cost of $|1024 + 160| = 1184$ bits. On the other hand, in the proposed LPPDA the DAP sends the message $M_2 = \{C_2, C_3, C_T^{agg}, X_d, \sigma_2, t_d\}$ to the OC which has the communication cost of $|C_2 + C_3 + C_T^{agg} + \sigma_2 + X_d + t_d| = 160 + 160 + 160 + 160 + 160 + 32 = 832$ bits.

Based on the comparison values of the concerned schemes summarized in Table 6, we obtain the graphical representation in Fig. 3 to show the performance of the proposed scheme.

Table 6. Communication cost of SM-DAP and DAP-OC transmissions

Scheme	SM-DAP	DAP-SM
[44]	1024	2659
[46]	2659	1024
[48]	704	704
[65]	544	1408
[61]	1184	1184
LPPDA	992	832

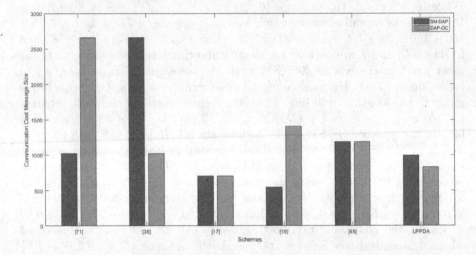

Fig. 3. Communication cost for the schemes.

Thus, from the analysis, the proposed LPPDA has an overall efficient communication cost to the related works as seen in Fig. 3 relative to the scheme in [48] in terms of SM-DAP communication segment cost while our scheme, LPPDA, has better merits overall the comparable schemes. In regards to the DAP-OC communication segment, our scheme has an efficient bandwidth load of 832 bits which providing desirable security requirements. Therefore, from the performance evaluation, in general our scheme is lightweight in both computation cost and communication cost, making it an ideal security scheme in a complex communication based network environment as that of smart grid.

Remark: By considering pre-computed operations, the overall communication and computation performance efficiency of LPPDA scheme surpasses that of relevant related works with a significant margin. The performance of the proposed work is achieved with a great advantage comparatively, as much as twice to the better performing scheme, while achieving user anonymity without sacrificing computation efficiency.

This work is on going and we will progressively devote on including other versatile security techniques that ensure a robust modern grid with its applications and functionalities. In our further works, multi-dimension data aggregation techniques will be considered, to ensure security, classification and uploading of different types of electrical appliance measurements data to the utility company. We consider incorporating a privacy-preserving data aggregation focusing on a block-chain smart grid network environment and its functionality requirements. We also would endeavor to employ smart grid security schemes adaptive to dynamic machine learning based techniques in optimal scheduling and billing.

5   Conclusion

In this paper, we proposed a lightweight privacy-preserving data aggregation scheme based on elliptic cryptography, for smart grid communications. The framework is a two leveled architecture with the residential area data aggregator acting as an intermediate party between the smart meter and the utility service company. Unlike many other researches the proposed scheme protects user's real-time power consumption and identity from privacy and security breaches in an efficient manner by using a ECCDH problem in the encryption algorithm and additive homomorphic encryption. The comparison analysis shows that the scheme is efficient on overall system performance as well as robust in security, hence ideal for an IoT enhanced smart grid system. Our future work, related to this discipline will focus on secure and efficient multidimensional data preservation in smart grid network environment. Aspects of versatile technologies such as; block-chain, lattice cryptography and machine learning techniques will be considered, in order to realize a modern smart grid.

Acknowledgments. This research was possible because of the financial support from the World Bank, at the ACEIoT (African Center of Excellence in Internet of Things) which resides at the College of Science and Technology of the University of Rwanda, KN Street Nyarugenge, P.O. Box 3900, Kigali.

References

1. Abbasinezhad-Mood, D., Nikooghadam, M.: Design and hardware implementation of a security-enhanced elliptic curve cryptography based lightweight authentication scheme for smart grid communications. Futur. Gener. Comput. Syst. **84**, 47–57 (2018)
2. Abdallah, A., Shen, X.S.: A lightweight lattice-based homomorphic privacy-preserving data aggregation scheme for smart grid. IEEE Trans. Smart Grid **9**(1), 396–405 (2016)
3. Akyol, B.A., Kirkham, H., Clements, S.L., Hadley, M.D.: A survey of wireless communications for the electric power system. Technical report, Pacific Northwest National Lab (PNNL), Richland, WA, United States (2010)
4. Ali, I., Khan, E., Sabir, S.: Privacy-preserving data aggregation in resource-constrained sensor nodes in internet of things: a review. Future Comput. Inform. J. **3**(1), 41–50 (2018)

5. Alvarez-Alvarado, M.S., Jayaweera, D.: Reliability-based smart-maintenance model for power system generators. IET Gener. Trans. Distrib. **14**(9), 1770–1780 (2020)
6. Badra, M., Zeadally, S.: Lightweight and efficient privacy-preserving data aggregation approach for the smart grid. Ad Hoc Netw. **64**, 32–40 (2017)
7. Bae, M., Kim, K., Kim, H.: Preserving privacy and efficiency in data communication and aggregation for AMI network. J. Netw. Comput. Appl. **59**, 333–344 (2016)
8. Bao, H., Lu, R.: Comment on "privacy-enhanced data aggregation scheme against internal attackers in smart grid". IEEE Trans. Industr. Inf. **12**(1), 2–5 (2015)
9. Bekara, C.: Security issues and challenges for the IoT-based smart grid. In: FNC/MobiSPC, pp. 532–537 (2014)
10. Boudia, O.R.M., Senouci, S.M., Feham, M.: Elliptic curve-based secure multi-dimensional aggregation for smart grid communications. IEEE Sens. J. **17**(23), 7750–7757 (2017)
11. Chim, T.W., Yiu, S.M., Hui, L.C., Li, V.O.: Pass: privacy-preserving authentication scheme for smart grid network. In: 2011 IEEE International Conference on Smart Grid Communications (SmartGridComm), pp. 196–201. IEEE (2011)
12. Chim, T.W., Yiu, S.M., Li, V.O., Hui, L.C., Zhong, J.: PRGA: privacy-preserving recording & gateway-assisted authentication of power usage information for smart grid. IEEE Trans. Dependable Secure Comput. **12**(1), 85–97 (2014)
13. Das, D., Rout, D.K.: Adaptive algorithm for optimal real-time pricing in cognitive radio enabled smart grid network. ETRI J. **42**, 585–595 (2020)
14. Deng, R., Xiao, G., Lu, R., Chen, J.: Fast distributed demand response with spatially and temporally coupled constraints in smart grid. IEEE Trans. Industr. Inf. **11**(6), 1597–1606 (2015)
15. Desai, S., Alhadad, R., Chilamkurti, N., Mahmood, A.: A survey of privacy preserving schemes in IoE enabled smart grid advanced metering infrastructure. Clust. Comput. **22**(1), 43–69 (2019). https://doi.org/10.1007/s10586-018-2820-9
16. Dong, X., Zhou, J., Alharbi, K., Lin, X., Cao, Z.: An elgamal-based efficient and privacy-preserving data aggregation scheme for smart grid. In: 2014 IEEE Global Communications Conference, pp. 4720–4725. IEEE (2014)
17. Dwork, C., Kenthapadi, K., McSherry, F., Mironov, I., Naor, M.: Our data, ourselves: privacy via distributed noise generation. In: Vaudenay, S. (ed.) EUROCRYPT 2006. LNCS, vol. 4004, pp. 486–503. Springer, Heidelberg (2006). https://doi.org/10.1007/11761679_29
18. Eissa, M.: New protection principle for smart grid with renewable energy sources integration using WiMAX centralized scheduling technology. Int. J. Electr. Power Energy Syst. **97**, 372–384 (2018)
19. Eissa, M., Ali, N.: Performance evaluation of IEEE 802.16 real time polling and unsolicited grant service scheduling for protecting transmission and sub-transmission systems with multi-terminals. Electric Power Syst. Res. **167**, 48–57 (2019)
20. Ekanayake, J.B., Jenkins, N., Liyanage, K., Wu, J., Yokoyama, A.: Smart Grid: Technology and Applications. Wiley, Hoboken (2012)
21. Erkin, Z., Troncoso-Pastoriza, J.R., Lagendijk, R.L., Pérez-González, F.: Privacy-preserving data aggregation in smart metering systems: an overview. IEEE Signal Process. Mag. **30**(2), 75–86 (2013)
22. Farash, M.S., Attari, M.A.: A secure and efficient identity-based authenticated key exchange protocol for mobile client-server networks. J. Supercomput. **69**(1), 395–411 (2014). https://doi.org/10.1007/s11227-014-1170-5

23. Ferrag, M.A.: EPEC: an efficient privacy-preserving energy consumption scheme for smart grid communications. Telecommun. Syst. **66**(4), 671–688 (2017). https://doi.org/10.1007/s11235-017-0315-2

24. Ferrag, M.A., Ahmim, A.: Security solutions and applied cryptography in smart grid communications. IGI Global (2016)

25. Ferrag, M.A., Maglaras, L.A., Janicke, H., Jiang, J., Shu, L.: A systematic review of data protection and privacy preservation schemes for smart grid communications. Sustain. Urban Areas **38**, 806–835 (2018)

26. FitzPatrick, G.J., Wollman, D.A.: NIST interoperability framework and action plans. In: IEEE PES General Meeting, pp. 1–4. IEEE (2010)

27. Ford, V., Siraj, A., Rahman, M.A.: Secure and efficient protection of consumer privacy in advanced metering infrastructure supporting fine-grained data analysis. J. Comput. Syst. Sci. **83**(1), 84–100 (2017)

28. Garcia, F.D., Jacobs, B.: Privacy-friendly energy-metering via homomorphic encryption. In: Cuellar, J., Lopez, J., Barthe, G., Pretschner, A. (eds.) STM 2010. LNCS, vol. 6710, pp. 226–238. Springer, Heidelberg (2011). https://doi.org/10.1007/978-3-642-22444-7_15

29. Goel, S., Hong, Y.: Security challenges in smart grid implementation. In: Goel, S., Hong, Y. (eds.) Smart Grid Security. SC, pp. 1–39. Springer, London (2015). https://doi.org/10.1007/978-1-4471-6663-4_1

30. Gong, Y., Cai, Y., Guo, Y., Fang, Y.: A privacy-preserving scheme for incentive-based demand response in the smart grid. IEEE Trans. Smart Grid **7**(3), 1304–1313 (2015)

31. Gope, P., Sikdar, B.: Lightweight and privacy-friendly spatial data aggregation for secure power supply and demand management in smart grids. IEEE Trans. Inf. Forensics Secur. **14**(6), 1554–1566 (2018)

32. He, D., Kumar, N., Zeadally, S., Vinel, A., Yang, L.T.: Efficient and privacy-preserving data aggregation scheme for smart grid against internal adversaries. IEEE Trans. Smart Grid **8**(5), 2411–2419 (2017)

33. He, D., Zeadally, S., Wang, H., Liu, Q.: Lightweight data aggregation scheme against internal attackers in smart grid using elliptic curve cryptography. Wireless Communications and Mobile Computing 2017 (2017)

34. Hu, C., Huo, Y., Ma, L., Liu, H., Deng, S., Feng, L.: An attribute-based secure and scalable scheme for data communications in smart grids. In: Ma, L., Khreishah, A., Zhang, Y., Yan, M. (eds.) WASA 2017. LNCS, vol. 10251, pp. 469–482. Springer, Cham (2017). https://doi.org/10.1007/978-3-319-60033-8_41

35. Humayed, A., Lin, J., Li, F., Luo, B.: Cyber-physical systems security-a survey. IEEE Internet Things J. **4**(6), 1802–1831 (2017)

36. Hur, J., Koo, D., Shin, Y.: Privacy-preserving smart metering with authentication in a smart grid. Appl. Sci. **5**(4), 1503–1527 (2015)

37. Jo, H.J., Kim, I.S., Lee, D.H.: Efficient and privacy-preserving metering protocols for smart grid systems. IEEE Trans. Smart Grid **7**(3), 1732–1742 (2015)

38. Koo, J., Lin, X., Bagchi, S.: RL-BLH: learning-based battery control for cost savings and privacy preservation for smart meters. In: 2017 47th Annual IEEE/IFIP International Conference on Dependable Systems and Networks (DSN), pp. 519–530. IEEE (2017)

39. Li, D., Aung, Z., Williams, J., Sanchez, A.: P3: privacy preservation protocol for automatic appliance control application in smart grid. IEEE Internet Things J. **1**(5), 414–429 (2014)

40. Li, S., Xue, K., Yang, Q., Hong, P.: PPMA: privacy-preserving multisubset data aggregation in smart grid. IEEE Trans. Industr. Inf. **14**(2), 462–471 (2017)

41. Liu, J.K., Yuen, T.H., Au, M.H., Susilo, W.: Improvements on an authentication scheme for vehicular sensor networks. Expert Syst. Appl. **41**(5), 2559–2564 (2014)
42. Liu, Y., Cheng, C., Gu, T., Jiang, T., Li, X.: A lightweight authenticated communication scheme for smart grid. IEEE Sens. J. **16**(3), 836–842 (2015)
43. Liu, Y., Guo, W., Fan, C.I., Chang, L., Cheng, C.: A practical privacy-preserving data aggregation (3PDA) scheme for smart grid. IEEE Trans. Industr. Inf. **15**(3), 1767–1774 (2018)
44. Lu, R., Alharbi, K., Lin, X., Huang, C.: A novel privacy-preserving set aggregation scheme for smart grid communications. In: 2015 IEEE Global Communications Conference (GLOBECOM), pp. 1–6. IEEE (2015)
45. Lu, R., Heung, K., Lashkari, A.H., Ghorbani, A.A.: A lightweight privacy-preserving data aggregation scheme for fog computing-enhanced IoT. IEEE Access **5**, 3302–3312 (2017)
46. Lu, R., Liang, X., Li, X., Lin, X., Shen, X.: EPPA: an efficient and privacy-preserving aggregation scheme for secure smart grid communications. IEEE Trans. Parallel Distrib. Syst. **23**(9), 1621–1631 (2012)
47. Mahmood, K., Chaudhry, S.A., Naqvi, H., Kumari, S., Li, X., Sangaiah, A.K.: An elliptic curve cryptography based lightweight authentication scheme for smart grid communication. Futur. Gener. Comput. Syst. **81**, 557–565 (2018)
48. Ming, Y., Zhang, X., Shen, X.: Efficient privacy-preserving multi-dimensional data aggregation scheme in smart grid. IEEE Access **7**, 32907–32921 (2019)
49. Molina-Markham, A., Shenoy, P., Fu, K., Cecchet, E., Irwin, D.: Private memoirs of a smart meter. In: Proceedings of the 2nd ACM Workshop on Embedded Sensing Systems For Energy-efficiency in Building, pp. 61–66 (2010)
50. Morello, R., Mukhopadhyay, S.C., Liu, Z., Slomovitz, D., Samantaray, S.R.: Advances on sensing technologies for smart cities and power grids: a review. IEEE Sens. J. **17**(23), 7596–7610 (2017)
51. Paillier, P.: Public-key cryptosystems based on composite degree residuosity classes. In: Stern, J. (ed.) EUROCRYPT 1999. LNCS, vol. 1592, pp. 223–238. Springer, Heidelberg (1999). https://doi.org/10.1007/3-540-48910-X_16
52. Pawar, A., Rahane, S.: Opportunities and challenges of wireless communication technologies for smart grid applications. Int. J. Comput. Netw. Wirel. Mobile Commun. (IJCNWMC) **3**(1), 289–296 (2013)
53. Phiri, K.K., Kim, H.: Linear secret sharing scheme with reduced number of polynomials. Secur. Commun. Netw. (2019)
54. Qu, H., Shang, P., Lin, X.J., Sun, L.: Cryptanalysis of a privacy-preserving smart metering scheme using linkable anonymous credential. IACR Cryptol. ePrint Arch. **2015**, 1066 (2015)
55. Rivest, R.L.: Cryptography. In: Algorithms and Complexity, pp. 717–755. Elsevier (1990)
56. Savaglio, C., Ganzha, M., Paprzycki, M., Bădică, C., Ivanović, M., Fortino, G.: Agent-based internet of things: State-of-the-art and research challenges. Futur. Gener. Comput. Syst. **102**, 1038–1053 (2020)
57. Saxena, N., Choi, B.J., Lu, R.: Authentication and authorization scheme for various user roles and devices in smart grid. IEEE Trans. Inf. Forensics Secur. **11**(5), 907–921 (2015)
58. Scott, M.: Multiprecision integer and rational arithmetic cryptographic library (2003)
59. Shen, H., Zhang, M., Shen, J.: Efficient privacy-preserving cube-data aggregation scheme for smart grids. IEEE Trans. Inf. Forensics Secur. **12**(6), 1369–1381 (2017)

60. Sultan, S.: Privacy-preserving metering in smart grid for billing, operational metering, and incentive-based schemes: a survey. Comput. Secur. **84**, 148–165 (2019)
61. Tahir, M., Khan, A., Hameed, A., Alam, M., Khan, M.K., Jabeen, F.: Towards a set aggregation-based data integrity scheme for smart grids. Ann. Telecommun. **72**(9–10), 551–561 (2017). https://doi.org/10.1007/s12243-017-0602-7
62. Tan, S., De, D., Song, W.Z., Yang, J., Das, S.K.: Survey of security advances in smart grid: a data driven approach. IEEE Commun. Surv. Tutor. **19**(1), 397–422 (2017)
63. Tonyali, S., Akkaya, K., Saputro, N., Uluagac, A.S., Nojoumian, M.: Privacy-preserving protocols for secure and reliable data aggregation in IoT-enabled smart metering systems. Futur. Gener. Comput. Syst. **78**, 547–557 (2018)
64. Ustun, T.S., Khan, R.H., Hadbah, A., Kalam, A.: An adaptive microgrid protection scheme based on a wide-area smart grid communications network. In: 2013 IEEE Latin-America Conference on Communications, pp. 1–5. IEEE (2013)
65. Vahedi, E., Bayat, M., Pakravan, M.R., Aref, M.R.: A secure ECC-based privacy preserving data aggregation scheme for smart grids. Comput. Netw. **129**, 28–36 (2017)
66. Vaidya, B., Makrakis, D., Mouftah, H.: Provisioning substation-level authentication in the smart grid networks. In: 2011-MILCOM 2011 Military Communications Conference, pp. 1189–1194. IEEE (2011)
67. Vallent, T.F., Hanyurwimfura, D., Mikeka, C.: Efficient certificate-less aggregate signature scheme with conditional privacy-preservation for vehicular ad hoc networks enhanced smart grid system. Sensors **21**(9), 2900 (2021)
68. Wu, D., Zhou, C.: Fault-tolerant and scalable key management for smart grid. IEEE Trans. Smart Grid **2**(2), 375–381 (2011)
69. Xia, J., Wang, Y.: Secure key distribution for the smart grid. IEEE Trans. Smart Grid **3**(3), 1437–1443 (2012)
70. Yun, M., Yuxin, B.: Research on the architecture and key technology of internet of things (IoT) applied on smart grid. In: 2010 International Conference on Advances in Energy Engineering, pp. 69–72. IEEE (2010)
71. Zuo, X., Li, L., Peng, H., Luo, S., Yang, Y.: Privacy-preserving multidimensional data aggregation scheme without trusted authority in smart grid. IEEE Syst. J. **15**(1), 395–406 (2020)

Design and Implementation of Distributed Image Recognition App with Federal Learning Techniques

Yu-Wei Chan[1], Bo-You Wu[2], Yi-Ming Huang[2], and Chao-Tung Yang[2,3](✉)

[1] Department of Information Management, Providence University, Taichung, Taiwan
ywchan@gm.pu.edu.tw
[2] Department of Computer Science, Tunghai University, No. 1727, Sec. 4, Taiwan Boulevard, Taichung 407224, Taiwan, ROC
{s07351035,s07351048,ctyang}@thu.edu.tw
[3] Research Center for Smart Sustainable Circular Economy, Tunghai University, No. 1727, Sec. 4, Taiwan Boulevard, Taichung 407224, Taiwan, ROC

Abstract. In recent years, machine learning technology has been widely used in many fields, such as smart transportation, smart healthcare, smart finance and smart cities. Although machine learning technology has brought people a lot of convenience, the privacy problem of user data has also emerged [1]. Considering that users are not necessarily willing to upload personal privacy data to the cloud for deep learning training, therefore, instead of consuming a lot of bandwidth to upload data to the cloud, it is better to train on the local device and then use the model parameters obtained after training. (For example: weights and bias, etc.) upload to the server for aggregation. This emerging machine learning technology is called federated learning. In this way, the privacy and security of data can be guaranteed, and the purpose of decentralized learning can be achieved through aggregation. This study uses the architecture of federated learning technology and convolutional neural network algorithms to implement distributed image recognition mobile applications. This application allows users to use their mobile devices and the central servers for repeated training. After multiple rounds of repeated training, the convergence will be stabilized, and the accuracy will be significantly improved. At the same time, it can take into account privacy and achieve the machine the purpose of learning.

Keywords: Federated learning · Convolutional neural network · Image recognition · Decentralized deep learning · Machine learning

1 Introduction

In recent years, with the emerging development of artificial intelligence (AI) technology, deep learning (DL) technology has become a popular branch in the field of machine learning [2]. Deep learning technology has been successfully used in various fields, such

Y.-B. Lin et al. (Eds.): SGIoT 2021, LNICST 447, pp. 98–110, 2022.
https://doi.org/10.1007/978-3-031-20398-5_8

as image recognition[3], action recognition[4], speech recognition[5], natural language processing (NLP)[6] and network applications[7].

In the traditional machine learning architecture, a central server manages the trained model. First, the sensors or edge devices return the collected data to the server and perform training in the server, and then send the training results to the edge devices or mobile devices. However, this method will cause data privacy and security problems, and will occupy a large amount of network bandwidth and results in network delay problems. To solve the above mentioned problems, Federated Learning (FL) approach has been proposed [8, 9]. In the FL approach, the central server is connected with each client device (edge device/mobile device), and the client devices use local data to training for building a model, and then send the model weights obtained after training back to the central server for aggregation [10]. In the process of model training, there is no need to send clients' data back to the server. Thus, the FL approach can solve the problem of data privacy of users while it can achieve the accuracy similar to that of a centralized machine learning architecture.

Currently, there are many applications using federated learning technology. For example, if multiple hospitals want to cooperate to train a model, but because the patient's private information is not convenient to provide to other hospitals, through the framework of federated learning technology, machine learning training is performed in each hospital before the training. The latter weights are provided to the central server. In addition, Google's own input method Gboard allows each user's mobile phone to download a set of models, and then train the local model according to the user's usage behavior, and then send it back to the central server so that the user's input words will be sent back to Google, and the candidate words can appear more accurately. The voice assistant Siri on the iPhone, through the neural network engine on the CPU, allows the phone to train the user's voice, and the audio recorded by Siri never leaves the local device.

The purpose of this study is to implement the development of image recognition apps by using the federated learning technology, such that users can use their mobile devices for training to perform image recognition applications while ensure the data privacy of users.

2   Background Review and Related Works

In this section, we review some background knowledges for later use of system design and implementation. Several techniques which are applied as the methods in this work, such as federated learning, convolutional neural networks (CNNs) and Kotlin are introduced in the following.

2.1   Federated Learning

Federal learning is a decentralized machine learning architecture proposed by Google in 2016 [8]. This architecture is composed of a central server and multiple client devices that participate in training in different places. The client devices first train with their own data, and then upload their respective model weights to the central server after the training, and then the central aggregates the weights. Repeat the above steps until convergence is reached. The architecture is performed in the form of client-server, in which each client uses local data for training, and then uploads the updated model parameters to the server, so as to optimize all models simultaneously. Thus, even if the information can not be shared, the learning strategy still can be carried out by taking into account the problems of privacy and model bias [9].

The central server will update the global model based on the aggregated results, and return the updated global model to the clients participating in the FL architecture. The clients will update their local model and start the next round training. At the same time, the performance metrics of the overall model will be evaluated. When the performance metrics are converged to be stable, the iterative training of the FL model will be terminated.

2.2 Convolutional Neural Networks

Convolutional Neural Network (CNN) is a backforward neural network. Its artificial neurons can respond to a part of the surrounding units in the coverage area, which is excellent for large-scale image processing. It has two important characteristics [11]: (1). It can effectively reduce a large amount of data to a small amount of data, (2). It can effectively retain the characteristics of the image, in line with the principles of image processing.

2.3 Kotlin

Kotlin is a programming language developed by JetBrains. It is a statically typed programming language that runs on the Java Virtual Machine (JVM). It can be compiled into Java byte code, or it can be converted into using LLVM after compilation. It also provides native codes to execute, or compile into JavaScript language for browser to execute.

3 Background Review and Related Works

The overall architecture of this work is shown in Fig. 1. The system is mainly divided into two parts: the first one is the server side, and the second one is the client side. First, on the server side, the system uses Kotlin as the main programming language. The server side is mainly responsible for generating an initialized global model, and then sending the global model to each connected client. After the client receives the initialized global model, it trains with the model and then uploads the updated model weights to the server. After receiving the weights obtained from clients, the weights obtained by each client are aggregated to generate an updated global model, and then the updated global model is transmitted to the clients. The second part is the client side, which is mainly built in the Android operating system and uses Kotlin as the main App programming language. In addition, the DeepLearning4j software is deployed as the machine learning framework. The image recognition training will be performed on the client device itself, and then the related weights of the recognition images will be uploaded to the server.

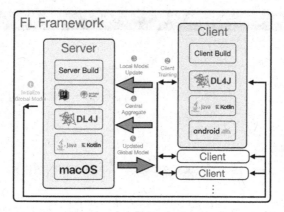

Fig. 1. The system architecture.

With regard to the server design and implementation of the system, the server is mainly responsible for starting a new round and accepting the weight of the client's return. In the system, we set a port and can use the browser to check whether the server is normal operation, its setting code is shown in Fig. 2. In addition, the server also needs to train the weights sent from the client. In this system, we place the model in the newly created main folder, which contains the weight of the client (currentRound), and the training is completed. The sub-folder of the model, and during training, the Server will read the parameter update file from the currentRound for training, and it can also open the DL4J UI interface to view the training process and results (as shown in Fig. 3).

```java
import org.eclipse.jetty.server.Server;
import org.eclipse.jetty.servlet.ServletContextHandler;
import org.eclipse.jetty.servlet.ServletHolder;
import org.glassfish.jersey.media.multipart.MultiPartFeature;
import org.glassfish.jersey.server.ResourceConfig;
import org.glassfish.jersey.servlet.ServletContainer;

public class JobQueueServer {

    public static void main(String[] args) {

        final ResourceConfig resourceConfig = new ResourceConfig(RestService.class);
        resourceConfig.register(MultiPartFeature.class);

        ServletHolder jerseyServlet = new ServletHolder(new ServletContainer(resourceConfig));

        Server jettyServer = new Server(9997);
        ServletContextHandler context = new ServletContextHandler(jettyServer, "/");
        context.addServlet(jerseyServlet, "/*");

        try {
            jettyServer.start();
            jettyServer.join();
        } catch (Exception e) {
            e.printStackTrace();
        } finally {
            jettyServer.destroy();
        }
    }
}
```

Fig. 2. The code of server establishment.

In addition, with regard to the client system design and implementation, the system uses an Android phone as the client side, it will accept the model from the server, and then perform CNN training. After performing the images recognition, the obtained weights will be transmitted back to the server, instead of transmitting the raw image data.

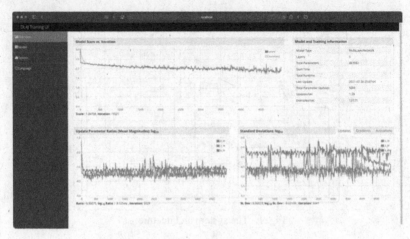

Fig. 3. The dashboard running in the server.

4   Experimental Results

4.1   The Hardware and Software Environment

The development software and hardware environment of this system is shown in Table 1. The system uses Android Studio IDE for server and mobile phone applications development. In addition, we use AVD emulator for application testing and execution in the system.

Table 1. The hardware and software equipment.

Hardware	**Server Side:** (1) Device: MacBook Pro (2) Operating System: MacOS 11.4 (3) CPU: Intel® Core™ i7-7820HQ 2.9 GHz (4) Memory (RAM): 16 GB (5) Hard Disk: 512 GB **Client Side:** (1) Device: Android Virtual Device Google Pixel 4 XL (2) Operating System: Android 10 (3) CPU: 4 Core CPU (4) Memory (RAM): 8 GB (5) Hard Disk: 20 GB
Software	(1) Programming Language: Kotlin v1.3.20 (JAVA v1.8.0) (2) Integrated Development Environment: Android Studio v4.1.3, IntelliJ IDEA 2020.2.4 (Community Edition)

4.2 Datasets

In this work, we use the Cifar-10 dataset [12] as the training and testing dataset for the development of the system. The dataset mainly consists of 10 categories of images which are all presented in the form of 32 × 32 pixels (as shown in Fig. 4). The categories are the airplanes, cars, birds, cats, deer, dogs, frogs, horses, boats, and trucks. The dataset contains a total of 60,000 images, each category contains 6,000 pictures, of which 50,000 pictures are used as the training set and 10,000 are used as the testing set. It is a collection of images often used in machine learning.

Fig. 4. The Cifar-10 dataset [12].

4.3 Implementation of App System

This app we develop will firstly use the camera software to capture images, recognize them and then store the classification results in the dataset for use in the next round of training. The obtained weights are then sent back to the server for training. In the following, we will present the main functions of the developed App system.

- The main screen of the system:

    The snapshot of the main screen in the system is shown in Fig. 5. From the figure, we see that when the model is loaded correctly, the program will pop up a prompt stating that "the model has been loaded". When the model has been loaded, the the toolbar ✿icon will appear in the upper right corner of the screen, which means that you can use the previously captured images for training. You can also directly click " ⬛ " to capture an image.

- The preliminary recognition function of the system:

    After the image is captured, the application will perform a preliminary recognition and will display which category the image belongs to. The snapshot of recognition results of the system is shown in Fig. 6. The user can choose whether to continue training or save the images. If you want to continue training, click " ![] ". If you want to save the image, click " ![] " to save the classification results.

Fig. 5. The snapshot of the main screen of the system.

Fig. 6. The snapshot of preliminary recognition results of the system.

- The model training function of the system:

  After the images are taken, all the images are trained by the CNN model. The model has a total of four layers, and its architecture is shown in Fig. 7. In the system, we set the number of training (Epoch) to 100.

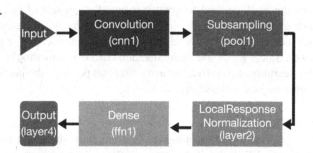

Fig. 7. The CNN model architecture used in this system.

Figure 8 is the snapshot of the model training in the system. From the figure, we see that the system provides the training data, model parameters and other related information. In addition, the training accuracy record of iterations are shown in the system.

Fig. 8. The snapshot of model training process.

In the CNN layer in the system, we use Adam's optimizer to update the weights of the neural network. The advantages are high computational efficiency and small memory requirements, and the ReLU activation function is used to solve the problem of the disappearance of the gradient, and to greatly reduce the amount of calculation. The pooling layer mainly adopts the MaxPooling method, such that when the entire image is shifted, the pixel judgment will not cause any influence which means that it has a good anti-noise function. Local Response Normalization (LRN) is a method to improve the accuracy of deep learning, generally after activation and pooling, the purpose of use is to reduce the error rate of the classifier.

When the training is finished, that indicates that the message "Model training completed" will be shown in the system (as shown in Fig. 9). Then, press the return button to show the recognition results. When the clients transmit the weight parameters to the server, the app will show the completed trained model which has been uploaded to the server (as shown in Fig. 10).

Fig. 9. The snapshot of model training completion.

Fig. 10. The completed trained model uploaded to the server side.

After the first round of training, the images will be recognized. Then, the classification accuracy rate with respect to each category will be obtained. From Fig. 6, we see that the accuracy rate of the initial recognition with respect to each category are presented: 24% for Dog images, 16% for Cat images, 15% for Bird images, and so on. After multiple rounds of training, as shown in Fig. 11, the accuracy rate with respect to the Dog images is increased to 97%. From the implementation results, we see that after multiple rounds of training, the recognition results will tend to stabilize and converge. In addition, the accuracy rate will also be significantly increased.

- The server functions:

    In this work, we use the DL4J UI API [13] to provide an user interface in the browser to visualize the current network status and training process. First, in terms of model scores and iterative graphs which are shown in Fig. 12, the horizontal axis is the iteration, and the vertical axis is the model score. The trend of the number line in the figure increases with the iterations. Since we use the small batch gradient descent method, the model score is getting lower, and the fluctuations become smaller. In addition, the number line tends to converge, which means that the model training is more stable.

Fig. 11. The snapshot of accuracy results with respect to the dog images after multiple rounds of training.

Fig. 12. The snapshot of the obtained model score of the system.

Figure 13 shows the updated parameter ratio. In the figure, the horizontal axis is the iteration and the vertical axis is the logarithm of parameter ratios. From the figure, we see that after the iteration starts at 50, the value tends to be stable, and there does not have more fluctuations.

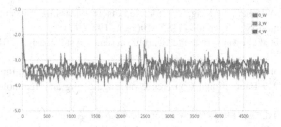

Fig. 13. The snapshot of the updated parameter ratio of the system.

5   Conclusion

In this work, we have successfully developed the App system based on the federated learning technology to perform real time image recognition with CNN models on the users' phones, and then returned the weight parameters after training to the central server for optimization. From the implementation results, we found that compared to the traditional machine learning approaches, the federated learning approach did not send raw images back to the server for model training. The implemented app let users to use their mobile devices and the central servers for iterative training. After multiple rounds of training, the convergence will be stabilized, and the accuracy will be significantly improved. Thus, the privacy issues of users could be solved and the amount of data transmission between the clients and the server could also be reduced significantly.

Acknowledgement. This work was supported in part by the Ministry of Science and Technology, Taiwan, under Grant MOST 110-2621-M-029-003-, 110-2221-E-029-002-MY3, 110-2221-E-126-004- and 110-2622-E-029-003-.

References

1. Mohassel, P., Zhang, Y.: Secureml: A system for scalable privacy-preserving machine learning. Proc. of the 2017 IEEE symposium on security and privacy (May 2017)
2. LeCun, Y., Bengio, Y., Hinton, G.: Deep learning. Nature **521**(7553) (2015)
3. He, K., Zhang, X., Ren, S., Sun, J.: Deep residual learning for image recognition. In: Proc. of the IEEE conference on computer vision and pattern recognition (CVPR) (June 2016)
4. Cao, Z., Hidalgo, G., Simon, T., Wei, S.-E., Sheikh, Y.: OpenPose: Realtime Multi-Person 2D Pose Estimation Using Part Affinity Fields. In: IEEE Transactions on Pattern Analysis and Machine Intelligence **43**(1), pp. 172–186 (1 Jan. 2021)
5. Xiong, W., Wu, L., Alleva, F., Droppo, J., Huang, X., Stolcke, A.: The Microsoft 2017 conversational speech recognition system. In: Proc. of 2018 IEEE International Conference on Acoustics, Speech and Signal Processing (ICASSP) (April 2018)
6. Young, T., Hazarika, D., Poria, S., Cambria, E.: Recent trends in deep learning based natural language processing. IEEE Comput. Intell. Mag. **13**(3), 55–75 (2018)
7. Qian, M., Fei, H., Hao, Q.: Deep learning for intelligent wireless networks: a comprehensive survey. IEEE Communications Surveys & Tutorials **20**(4), 2595–2621 (2018)
8. Konečný, J., McMahan, H.B., Yu, F.X., Richtárik, P., Suresh, A.T., Bacon, D.: Federated learning: Strategies for improving communication efficiency (2016). arXiv preprint arXiv: 1610.05492

9. Yang, Q., Liu, Y., Chen, T., Tong, Y.: Federated machine learning: concept and applications. ACM Trans. Intell. Sys. Technol. (TIST) **10**(2), 1–19 (2019)

10. Bonawitz, K., et al.: Towards federated learning at scale: System design (2019). arXiv preprint arXiv:1902.01046

11. Albawi, S., Mohammed, T.A., Al-Zawi, S.: Understanding of a convolutional neural network. In: Proc. of 2017 International Conference on Engineering and Technology (ICET) (Aug. 2017)

12. The CIFAR-10 dataset https://www.cs.toronto.edu/~kriz/cifar.html

13. Visualization - Deeplearning4j, https://deeplearning4j.konduit.ai/tuning-and-training/visualization

Improving Vision Clarity and Object Detection Accuracy in Heavy Rain Base on Neural Network

Chi Han Chen, Chien Hung Wu, Cheng Jun Wu, and Rung Shiang Cheng[✉]

Overseas Chinese University, Taichung, Taiwan
rscheng@ocu.edu.tw

Abstract. In heavy rain situation, clarity of both human vision and computer vision are significantly reduced. Rain removal GAN network is developed to resolve this problem. However, we find that this kind of network causes the decreasing of detection accuracy. In this work, we analysis the performance and the propose a detection network to get higher accuracy. Through the comparison of experimental results, our method can improve the IOU accuracy and detect confidence.

Keywords: Generative Adversarial Network(GAN) · Intersection over Union(IoU) · Non-Maximum suppression · Object detection · Self-driving car

1 Introduction

With the rapid development of technology, Artificial Intelligence (AI), Computer Vision (CV) have many applications in industry, medical treatment, and road driving, Under the response of different industries, the combined technology of the two gradually replaced a lot of manpower consume, have begun to popularize the use of artificial intelligence in many industrial chains or daily life applications.

With technology gradually replacing manpower, many technologies have begun to pursue convenience and safety. Under related topics, various problems of self-driving cars have been raised one by one, especially safety issues. It is safer for humans to judge the road conditions by human eyes compared to automatic assisted driving vehicles. In the accident record [1], the cause of the failure of the self-driving car may occur in a complex or the poor sight environment, but self-driving cars can operate well on road planning with systematic structure, it can be seen that in an environment where the route is not planned, autonomous driving is not completely reliable. The "human eye" is the most important factor of judgment when people are under normal conditions.

By [2] the author expressed the widely used rainfall image formation model as a rainfall. It is extended to convert the visible rain streaks (R) into a binary mask, use 0 and 1 to judge the presence or absence of rainfall area, keep good background details. In the real world, however, the accumulation of rainwater caused by heavy rain (rain

Y.-B. Lin et al. (Eds.): SGIoT 2021, LNICST 447, pp. 111–116, 2022.
https://doi.org/10.1007/978-3-031-20398-5_9

pattern overlap) is ignored. Taking atmospheric light factors into consideration, bring in the neural network to restore the image to a clean image. Although the rain can be removed by this method, but the output fake image make object detection sometimes failed.

In this work, we apply object detection with and without rain removal network respectively. Then, analysis the cause of miss detection and false detection of object detection cases. Base on the analysis, we implement an approach to combine rain removal network and object detection network into an assemble that can both output a clear image for human vision and higher accurate detection result base on object detection.

2 Related Works

2.1 Object Detection

1. With the development of neural networks, CNN is not purely for application in label classification applications. Therefore, [3] aims to make R-CNN perform better in terms of speed and accuracy by modifying the operation sequence and structural is-sues, simplifying the model design, and increasing the calculation speed. A picture only needs to be convolved once, saving a lot of computing and hardware resources, and using a multi-objective loss function, so that the original R-CNN multi-layer training becomes a simple backpropagation. After experimenting, Fast R-CNN mAP is also slightly higher than R-CNN the speed of training has also increased by nearly 9 times.

2. Use a two stage approach in the technique of [3]. Due to them all need to get regional suggestions first to locate the object, and then identify. In the [4] technique, the object recognition is regarded as the network structure of the regression problem. Based on one stage network architecture. After the image is input to the network, the corresponding object position and category will be directly output.

2.2 Image Restoration

3. In [5], it is introduced that the light reaches the video equipment, will be scattered by the atmosphere, resulting in poor image contrast. In bad weather, even if the image contrast is restored, but the image will still be blocked by natural factors such as fog and rain, there are still occlusion factors in the image. A physical model based on blurred images [6], propose an adaptive enhancement of a single image, to suppress the halo phenomenon caused by aerial removal, through the concept of adjacent pixel depth information, the concept of effective edge strength is given based on the perceived difference, a method to calculate the dephasing rate due to the entire image using the effective edge strength is proposed. Research [7] explains that time will not be covered by rain. Since rain removal model based on the morphological component analysis is been published [8], the image is decomposed into high and low frequencies [9], performs sparse coding and dictionary learning, restores the rain image to a clean image.

4. In [10] according to the framework proposed by [2]. The extension of the rain image is divided into high frequency images and low frequency images, input the rain image to the recursive ResNet [11], through the Guided Filtering Layer structure proposed

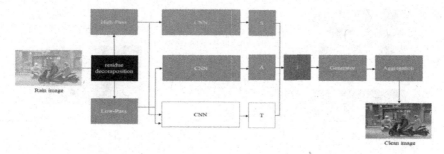

Fig. 1. Schematic diagram of rain removal network architecture

Table 1. Comparison of the accuracy of object etection in HeavyRainRemoval image

	Rain removal image	Rain image
Recognition rate is reduced, recognition error		
Increased recognition rate		

by [12], the exported high and low frequency images are brought into neural network training (Fig. 1). Finally, output the rain restoration image.

Even through technologies such as image restoration and restoration, but the photo has a gap with the real scene. Because this is a fake photo produced by repairing and restoring technology, may be different from the original image features, the object that causes the accuracy of object detection to decrease or to identify the wrong object (Table 1).

3 Methods

3.1 Networks

We experimented with System structure and Our method inference (Fig. 2). Tried to improve rain removal IOU accuracy.

3.2 Obtaining Rain and Restoring Street Images

Based on the collected rain image dataset. For image filtering that is not a street or pure natural scenery. Then filter the images that do not match object to be identified, speed

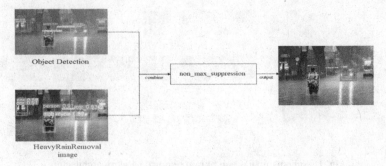

Fig. 2. Our method inference

up the next step of object annotation. Input the image into the rain removal model. Get the rain removal image.

3.3 Tracking Object Recognition Accuracy

Bring the rain image and rain removal image into object detection to predictions first. Through observing the result whether as expected. But even after rain removal. The human eye can improve the image recognition of the object. For computer vision feel it's not good. The result is not as good as expected (Table 1) as shown.

4 Result

There we can filter low confidence bounding boxes with Non-Maximum Suppression algorithm to reduce error detections to improve accuracy (Fig. 3) (Fig. 4).

Fig 3.1. (3.1.a) Detect duplicate people and locomotives. (3.1.b) The accuracy of detecting people is somewhat lower than (3.1.a). (3.1.c) solves the problem of detecting duplication and obtaining the best object bounding box.

Fig 3.2. (3.2.b) Multiple duplicates are detected. (3.2.c) Remove duplicate detections in the rain removal image and detect the correct person.

Fig. 3. YOLO, HeavyRainRemoval, our method Compare

Fig. 4. Ours method result: combine the images of the two methods through our proposed method. After Non-Maximum Suppression, the resulting images are more accurate

5 Conclusions

According to the experimental results, the accuracy of the image after rain removal in the object recognition not entirely better than images with rain. Extract the bounding box of the two images through Non-Maximum Suppression. The best recognized bounding box and confidence can be obtained between the two images. Make up for the identification error between the two. This method can effectively reduce misjudgments. Improve the accuracy of object recognition.

Acknowledgements. The authors would like to thank the National Science Council, Taiwan, R.O.C. for financially supporting this research under Contract No. NSC MOST 109-2221-E-240 -002 -MY3, MOST 110-2622-E-240 -002, 110-2813-C-240 -004 -E.

References

1. Tian, Y., Pei, K., Jana, S., Ray, B.: Deeptest: automated testing of deep-neural-network-driven autonomous cars (2017). arXiv preprint arXiv:1708.08559
2. Yang, W., Tan, R., Feng, J., Liu, J., Guo, Z., Yan, S.: Oint Rain Detection and Removal via Iterative Region Dependent Multi-Task Learning
3. Girshick, R.: Fast R-CNN. IEEE International Conference on Computer Vision (ICCV) **2015**, 1440–1448 (2015). https://doi.org/10.1109/ICCV.2015.169
4. Redmon, J., Divvala, S., Girshick, R., Farhadi, A.: You only look once: unified, real-time object detection. In: 2016 IEEE Conference on Computer Vision and Pattern Recognition (CVPR), Las Vegas, NV, pp. 779–788 (2016). https://doi.org/10.1109/CVPR.2016.91
5. Narasimhan, S.G., Nayar, S.K.: Contrast restoration of weather degraded images. IEEE Trans. Pattern Anal. Mach. Intell. **25**(6), 713–724 (2003). https://doi.org/10.1109/TPAMI.2003.120 1821. June
6. Yao, B., Huang, L., Liu, C.: Adaptive defogging of a single image second international symposium on computational intelligence and design. Changsha **2009**, 56–59 (2009). https://doi.org/10.1109/ISCID.2009.21
7. Zhang, X., Li, H., Qi, Y., Leow, W.K., Ng, T.K.: Rain removal in video by combining temporal and chromatic properties. In: 2006 IEEE International Conference on Multimedia and Expo, Toronto, Ont., pp. 461–464 (2006). https://doi.org/10.1109/ICME.2006.262572

8. Kang, L.W., Lin, C.W., Fu, Y.H.: Automatic singleimage-based rain streaks removal via image decomposition. IEEE Trans. Image Process. **21**(4), 1742–1755 (2012). April
9. Bobin, J., Starck, J.L., Fadili, J.M., Moudden, Y., Donoho, D.L.: Morphological component analysis: an adaptive thresholding strategy. IEEE Trans Image Process. **16**(11), 2675–2681 (2007). Nov.
10. Li, R., Cheong, L., Tan, R.T.: Heavy rain image restoration: integrating physics model and conditional adversarial learning. In: 2019 IEEE/CVF Conference on Computer Vision and Pattern Recognition (CVPR), Long Beach, CA, USA, pp. 1633–1642 (2019). https://doi.org/10.1109/CVPR.2019.00173
11. Yang, W., et al.: Deep edge guided recurrent residual learning for image super-resolution. IEEE Trans. Image Process. **26**(12), 5895–5907 (2017). https://doi.org/10.1109/TIP.2017.2750403. Dec.
12. Kingma, D.P., Ba, J.: Adam: a method for stochastic optimization. CoRR, abs/1412.6980 (2014)

An Enhanced Location-Data Differential Privacy Protection Method Based on Filter

Shasha Zhang[1], Haiyan Kang[2(✉)], and Dong Yu[2]

[1] School of Computer Science, Beijing Information Science and Technology University,
Beijing 100192, China
[2] School of Information Management, Beijing Information Science and Technology University,
Beijing 100192, China
kanghaiyan@126.com

Abstract. Location based service (LBS) is the basic function and important application of Internet of things. The disclosure of location data which contains a lot of sensitive information will be a threat for individual. This paper proposed an enhanced location-data differential privacy protection method based on filter. Firstly, noise is added in location-data for differential privacy. Secondly, Kalman is used to predict, correct and optimize the Location-data after the addition of noise, which ensure the optimization to satisfy the differential privacy. Finally, released the processed data and carry out the location query service. Experimental results demonstrate that the proposed algorithm promotes Location-data utility and level of privacy protection.

Keywords: Privacy protection · Kalman filter · Location-data · Location based service · Differential privacy

1 Introduction

The Internet of things (IoT) is a new concept proposed in recent years, which is getting more and more attention. The Internet of things has been widely used, covering such as intelligent transportation, environmental protection, government work, public safety, environmental monitoring and so on. However, the Internet of things faces many security threats at the same time. It is one of the necessary conditions for the wide application to solve the problem of privacy protection in the application of the IoT.

Location based service (LBS) is the basic function and important application of Internet of things. In recent years, the applications and offline products with location-based services as the core are becoming more and more popular. Such as: Hand ring, Runtopia APP, Baidu Map, etc. These sensors and mobile terminals with "inner smart" query the location data and provide it to the server. This provides more extension services to users. However, when users share their location information to the Internet of things for extended service, the location privacy information would be threatened. The query scenario based on the location service is shown in Fig. 1.

© ICST Institute for Computer Sciences, Social Informatics and Telecommunications Engineering 2022
Published by Springer Nature Switzerland AG 2022. All Rights Reserved
Y.-B. Lin et al. (Eds.): SGIoT 2021, LNICST 447, pp. 117–127, 2022.
https://doi.org/10.1007/978-3-031-20398-5_10

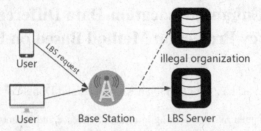

Fig. 1. Query scenarios based on location service

The location data privacy threat means that the location data of the user is stolen by the location transmission device, the location information transmission channel without authorization and so on. An attacker can combine the user location information in the Internet of things with extension services to infer the information of a user, such as personal habits, home addresses, private life or identify a person's true identity through existing background knowledge. Forester Research has conducted a more authoritative sample of private placement in the United States. The result shows that 70% of users think it is necessary to pass legislation to guarantee the privacy of their location. The threat of location data privacy security seriously hinders the market development and commercial prospects of location services. Therefore, it is very important to keep confidential the location information of users while providing services to users.

Currently, most of the privacy-preserving approaches in location-based services are based on k-anonymity or l-diversity [1], and such techniques generalize the user's real location into a region to achieve privacy protection of location information. These approaches provide low precision and large amount of location data to the server, which obviously degrades the quality of service. Dwork et al. [2] proposed a differential privacy-preserving model in 2006, which became a mainstream technique due to its good privacy-preserving strength, by adding random noise to the original query result so that adding or removing a piece of data in the dataset has no effect on the query result, thus making it is difficult for an attacker to infer a particular piece of real data back through multiple queries to achieve privacy protection. However, although existing differential privacy solutions enhance the protection of location data to some extent, the setting of differential privacy noise size can lead to degradation of service quality of service providers.

The main contributions of this paper are as follows: (1) An enhanced location data differential privacy protection algorithm based on filtering technology is proposed. (2) The Kalman filtering mechanism is introduced to optimize the data of differential privacy protection. Thus, the location information obtained by the server is more accurate and the quality of the location service is improved. At the same time, privacy is not disclosed.

2   Related Work

The literature [3–5] proposed a location-based privacy protection technology based on k-anonymity. The position scope of the user is given by generalization to prevent the real location of the user from being exposed. Any location in the position scope could be the user's real location, so the user's real location is protected. However, if the generalization is too large, it will reduce the quality of the location service. C. Y. Chow et al. [6] proposed a k-anonymity protection method of introducing an anonymous device. Not only can this method prevent user location information from being leaked, but also prevent user identity information from being leaked. But this approach increases the server's computing resources and the load on the network. Gedik and Liu [7] proposed that user-defined k values and minimize the size of fuzzy areas. However, this method has a large amount of computation, and the system is not very efficient, and it can only be used when the k value is small. Chen Ping, Feng Yunxia [8] proposed and implemented a mobile phone based location anonymization scheme for continuous query LBS users. The method adopts the independent system structure, and all the anonymous protection calculation is carried on the mobile terminal. Privacy protection can be achieved by constantly sending false queries, without a third party server providing anonymization service. But this method of sending fake inquiries does not have the effect of k-anonymity. And the constant sending of bogus queries not only increases the burden on the server, but also increases the load on the mobile network. Zhang et al. [9] proposed a scheme to enhance user privacy through caching and spatial anonymity in continuous LBS, using multi-level caching to reduce the risk of exposing user's information to untrusted location service providers, however, an attacker may obtain the user's true identity based on an inference attack to obtain a specific user's location. Zhao et al. [10] developed a trustworthiness-based k-anonymity scheme, where The trustworthiness is set based on the location similarity of the mobile user, and the computational overhead of the change scheme is large.

The literature [11] proposes a privacy-preserving algorithm for trajectory suppression based on information entropy, which calculates the minimum cost of suppressing sensitive location points through a function to select a reasonable suppression method for the sequences containing sensitive points in the original dataset. The scrambling technique is to generate false locations from real locations by certain transformations to achieve the purpose of protecting real locations. The literature [12] proposes a maximum-minimum false location selection scheme based on the false location privacy method, which makes it difficult for the attacker to combine the edge information to filter some false locations for privacy protection of location information. All the above privacy protection techniques have some limitations and drawbacks, and attackers can obtain users' location privacy information through long-term observation, mining and analysis [13–15], so these techniques cannot resist relevant attacks background knowledge attacks.

Dwork et al. [2] proposed a differential privacy-preserving model in 2006, which became a mainstream technique due to its good privacy-preserving strength, by adding random noise to the original query results so that adding or removing a piece of data in the dataset has no effect on the query results, thus making it difficult for an attacker to backpropagate a piece of real data through multiple queries to achieve privacy protection. Huo Zheng et al. [16] constructed noisy quadtrees and noisy R-trees for free space and road network space, respectively, and protected location data by adding Laplace noise, but did not consider the interaction between 2 consecutive moments of location data. Yin et al. [17] proposed a location privacy preservation method that satisfies differential privacy constraints to protect location data privacy and maximize the utility of data and algorithms in industrial IoT. Yan et al. [18] proposed an unbalanced quadtree partitioning algorithm based on region uniformity, and accordingly, designed a gradient privacy budget allocation scheme and adjustment method to ensure the effectiveness of the differential privacy model. Zhao et al. [19] combined federal learning and localized differential privacy together, and proposed four localized differential privacy mechanisms to scramble the gradients generated by vehicles, and introduced a three-output mechanism to reduce the communication cost. Tian Feng et al. [20] proposed a personalized differential privacy publishing mechanism for trajectory data, using Hilbert curve to extract the distribution characteristics of trajectory data at each moment to generate location clusters, using sampling mechanism and index mechanism to select the representative elements of each location cluster, and then using the location representative elements to generalize the original trajectory data to generate the trajectory data to be published.

3 Differential Privacy

3.1 Differential Privacy Conceptions

Definition 1. Differential Privacy [21]. A randomized algorithm K, Range(k) denotes the value Range of a random algorithm K, $Pr[z]$ denotes the disclosure risk of event z. For any two neighboring datasets D_1 and D_2, at most one record is different, namely, $|D_1 \Delta D_2|$. Algorithm K is ε-differential privacy if for any datasets D_1 and D_2 differing at most one record, and any possible outputs set D,

$$Pr[K(D_1) = D] \le e^\varepsilon \times Pr[K(D_2) = D] \qquad (1)$$

where ε is privacy parameter, also called the privacy budget, e is the natural base.

Definition 2. Global Sensitivity [22]. The global sensitivity of a function $f : D_n \to R^d$, is

$$\Delta f = max\|f(D_1) - f(D_2)K\|_P \qquad (2)$$

where, R is the real space of the mapping, d is the query dimension of function f, P is the norm distance measured by Δf.

3.2 Mechanisms to Achieving Differential Privacy

Laplace Mechanism
Typical differential privacy is implemented by adding a Laplace noise to the output of the query. It defined as follows.

Definition 3. Laplace Mechanism [22]. For a function $f : D_n \to R^d$, the mechanism satisfies ε-differential privacy, if the output results satisfy.

$$Y(D) = f(D) + Lap\left(\frac{\Delta f}{\varepsilon}\right) \qquad (3)$$

where Lap( ) is density function of Laplace.

Exponential Mechanism

For functions where adding noise does not make sense or the output space is non-numeric, the exponential mechanism was proposed by McSherry. This mechanism mainly deals with the non-numerical algorithm of the output results.

Definition 4. Exponential Mechanism [23]. For a score function $q : (D \times O) \rightarrow R$, the mechanisms K satisfies ε-differential privacy, if K satisfy.

$$K(D, u) = \{r : | \Pr[r \in O] \propto \exp\left(\frac{\varepsilon q(D, r)}{2\Delta q}\right)\} \tag{4}$$

If the mechanisms K that outputs r with probability proportional to $exp(\ )$.

4 Location Data Query Differential Privacy Protection Algorithm Based on Filter Mechanism

4.1 Location Data

The location data is the representation value of the original data in the dimension of the location. It is to project the spatially based spatial data into the two-dimensional plane of longitude and latitude representation. Location data query privacy protection means that users can freely query any other location data within the individual location dimension and ensure that the location information of the individual is not leaked.

Definition 5. Location data. Location data is a spatial data. We mapped the spatial location data to the two-dimensional space. Using two-dimensional spatial representation represents location data. Namely, we use $T(x, y)$ for the location data. The location data is only considered with the longitude and dimension of the position, where x and y is the longitude and latitude of position data.

4.2 Location Data Query Privacy Protection Mechanism

The process of differential privacy protection based on filter mechanism is shown in Fig. 2.

The process of the location data differential privacy protection algorithm based on filter mechanism is as follows:

(1) Differential privacy protection for location data p is achieved by adding Laplace noise.
(2) Use filtering technology to predict and revise the sampled data after adding noise. Because the Laplace noise value is randomly generated. There may be larger disturbances to the original location data. It makes the data less practical and affects the quality of query results.

(3) Use Kalman filtering technology to optimize the position data after adding noise. That ensures that the optimization is satisfied with the ε-differential privacy. Obtain the optimized query location data $\hat{p}$ and submit it to the location service provider. The location service provider provides location services based on query location data $\hat{p}$.

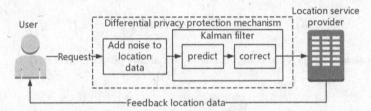

Fig. 2. The process of differential privacy protection based on filter mechanism

Use Kalman filter to predict and correct the location data after adding noise. It can obviously improve the availability of location data and improve the quality of location service. The differential privacy protection mechanism based on filter technology has obvious advantages for the practicality of location data, which will be proved in subsequent experiments.

4.3 Kalman Filtering Mechanism

Kalman filter [24] can be used to predict and modify the location data of noise, which can solve the problem of low service quality caused by adding noise better.

System measurement model:

$$Z = T + v \tag{5}$$

where, Z is the value of the location data T after adding noise. is Gaussian white noise (measurement noise). It's a Gaussian distribution that is expected of 0 and the variance is R:

$$v \sim N(0, R) \tag{6}$$

The system measurement model is very similar to the Laplace noise model, and the difference is that the noise value distribution obeys the Gaussian distribution and the Laplace distribution. Therefore, the Kalman filter can be used in differential privacy protection by using Gaussian noise to simulate the Laplace noise (i.e., the value of R). L. Fan et al. [25, 26] combined with the relevant formula of Kalman filtering, the optimal selection method of variance R is given, $R = 1/\varepsilon^2$, when using Gaussian noise to simulate the Laplace noise. The selection of this parameter will be proved in subsequent experiments.

The use of Kalman filtering in differential privacy is solved in the above text. The main function of Kalman filtering in this paper is to solve the problem of decreasing service quality of service providers due to differential privacy protection. Kalman filtering can reduce the noise value very well, so that the service provider can collect the posterior estimate of the actual location of the user and improve the service quality.

It is assumed that T means kalman prior estimates, $\hat{T}$ means the posterior estimate (the location data value service provider gets). The calculation equation of the posterior estimation in kalman filter is as follows:

$$\overline{T} = T \tag{7}$$

$$\hat{T} = \overline{T} + K_k(Z - \overline{T}) \tag{8}$$

According to the Eq. (8), the posterior estimate can be calculated. The user location data value is obtained by the service provider. It is determined by the sampling point data plus noise value Z, the prior estimator T and K_k. Where, K_k is the Kalman gain, which is constantly changing. Among them, K represents the Kalman gain, which is constantly changing. It minimizes the error and the variance.

Kalman filtering mechanism is the process of predicting and correcting the optimal estimation. Its obvious advantage is that the filtering principle takes into account all available data within the system (the original value and the noise value). The predicted values are the closest to the original data. It can make up for the inaccuracy of the differential privacy protection to the location data and ensure that the individual's true location privacy is not leaked. Subsequent experiments will demonstrate the advantages of using Kalman filtering technology for location data query protection.

Original location data is $T(x, y)$, total privacy budget is ε, distribution the total privacy budget average to each location data. The location data differential privacy protection algorithm based on the filtering mechanism is as follows:

Algorithm: Differential privacy protection algorithm for location data based on filtering mechanism

Input: $T(x, y)$-original location data, ε-privacy budget

Output: T -query location data

Step 1: Add noise to location data, obtain the value $Z_x = x + Lap\left(\frac{0,1}{\varepsilon^2}\right)$, $Z_y = y + Lap\left(\frac{0,1}{\varepsilon^2}\right)$

Step 2: Prediction: $\overline{x} = x$, correction: $\hat{x} = \overline{x} + K_k(Z_x - \overline{x})$

Step 3: Do the Same process for y

Step 4: Get the final query location data $\hat{T} = (\overline{x}, \overline{y})$

Step 5: Repeat Step 1–4. // The program continuously circulation process all the location information in the data set

---

5   Experimental Evaluation

5.1   Experimental Datasets and Environment

The experimental datasets come from a location service social network user accessing the location data from the Datatang [27]. It contains the location data of 270,000 longitude and latitude representations. To simplify the experiment, only ten percent of the data was sampled for comparison. The algorithm uses the Java language implementation, the programming environment is Eclipse8. The experimental environment is Windows7 2. 68 GHz, 4.0 GB, data mining tool is SQL Server 2008R2.

5.2 Validation of Parameter R Selection in Filter Mechanism

In the filter mechanism, the choice of parameter R directly affects the accuracy of the whole mechanism. It mentioned above that variance R of Gaussian noise has a certain relationship with the value of the Laplace noise ε. In this experiment, we compare the different values of R in terms of the privacy budget $\varepsilon = 0.1$, $\varepsilon = 0.01$, and then verify the value formula of optimal R. As shown in Fig. 3, the x axis represents the value of R. The y axis represents the relative error. Obviously, when the privacy budget $\varepsilon = 0.1$, $\varepsilon = 0.01$, the optimal value of R is $R = 10^2$ and $R = 10^4$. The formula of the optimal value of R is verified $R = 1/\varepsilon^2$.

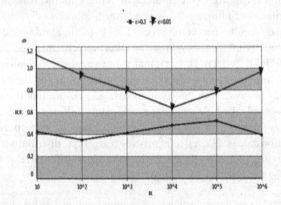

Fig. 3. Kalman filter parameter R selection

5.3 Experiment and Analysis

Experimental Steps: Firstly, use the location data differential privacy protection algorithm based on filter mechanism. Input: original location data $T(x, y)$ and privacy budget $\varepsilon = 1, 0.1, 0.01$. Lastly, output the final query location data $\hat{T}$.

Test and Analysis: IN order to verify the advantage of the data practicability, we compare the experiment with traditional differential privacy and noise technology. The privacy budget parameters were selected for comparison with $\varepsilon = 1, 0.1, 0.01$ respectively. The relative error between two protection mechanisms is obtained to judge the merits of the data availability. (When $\varepsilon = 0.1$, $\varepsilon = 0.01$, $\varepsilon = 1$, the data practicality of the three privacy budgets is quite similar and due to space reasons, this paper only gives a comparison of $\varepsilon = 1$), as shown in Fig. 4. Here red solid line represents our method(laplace + kalrman), and black dotted line represents traditional differential privacy (laplace).

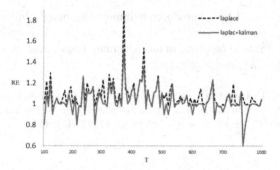

(a) Comparison of longitude data query values

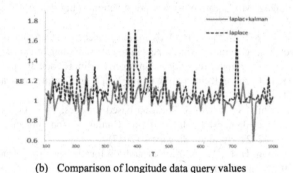

(b) Comparison of longitude data query values

Fig. 4. Comparison of the usability of the data after filter

Analysis: (1) In Fig. 4, the practical aspect of the position data treated with filtration technology is significantly higher than that of the noising mechanism. After filtering, the location data is closer to the original value, which can improve the service quality of the location service provider and enable users to query the service more accurately. Figure 4(a) and Fig. 4(b) are approximately overlapped, and the relative error is not obvious because the added noise value is too small and the optimized data optimization is not obvious. (2) In terms of data security, the two methods use differential privacy for protection. Data security is similar. (3) Based on the experiment, the data practicability and security of the location data differential privacy protection algorithm based on the filtering mechanism can achieve the optimal balance of differential privacy protection mechanism.

6   Conclusions

Location-based services can provide users with many conveniences and improve the user experience. But location services must require users to provide their own specific location information, which may pose a serious threat to users' privacy. In this paper, the differential privacy mechanism is applied to the location data query protection, and

Kalman filtering technology is introduced to improve the practicability of location data. It is to focus on practicality and user's location security. The experiments show that the protection mechanism proposed in this paper has a significant improvement in both practicality of data and privacy protection.

Acknowledgment. This work is partially supported by National Social Science Foundation of China (21BTQ079), Humanities and Social Sciences Project of the Ministry of Education (20YJAZH046) and Higher education research projects (2020GJZD02).

References

1. Wang, L., Xiaofeng, M.: Location privacy preservation in big data era: a survey. J. Softw. **25**(04), 693–712 (2014)
2. Dwork, C., Kenthapadi, K., McSherry, F., Mironov, I., Naor, M.: Our data, ourselves: privacy via distributed noise generation. In: Annual International Conference on the Theory and Applications of Cryptographic Techniques. Springer, Berlin, Heidelberg, pp. 486–503 (2006)
3. Kim, J.S., Li, K.J.: Location K-anonymity in indoor spaces. GeoInformatica **20**(3), 415–451 (2016)
4. Jagwani, P., Kaushik, S.: Privacy in location based services: Protection strategies, attack models and open challenges. In: International Conference on Information Science and Applications, pp. 12–21. Springer, Singapore (2017)
5. Wang, Y.-H., Zhang, H.-L., Yu, X.-Z.: Research on location privacy in mobile internet. J. Commun. **36**(9), 1–14 (2015)
6. Chow, C.Y., Mokbel, M.F.: The new Casper: a privacy aware location-based database server. In: Proceedings of the 23rd IEEE International Conference on Data Engineering, pp. 1499–1500 (2007)
7. Gedik, B., Liu, L.: A customizable k-anonymity model for protecting location privacy. In: ICDCS'05, pp. 620–629 (2005)
8. Chen, L., Feng, Y.-X., Dai, G.-J.: Mobile phone based trajectory anonymization of continuous query LBS users. Appl. Res. Comput. **28**(12), 4653–4656 (2011)
9. Zhang, S., Li, X., Tan, Z., Peng, T., Wang, G.: A caching and spatial K-anonymity driven privacy enhancement scheme in continuous location-based services. Futur. Gener. Comput. Syst. **94**, 40–50 (2019)
10. Zhao, P., et al.: ILLIA: Enabling k-anonymity-based privacy preserving against location injection attacks in continuous LBS queries. IEEE Internet Things J. **5**(2), 1033–1042 (2018)
11. Yifei, W., Luo Yonglong, Y., Qingying, L.Q., Wen, C.: A trajectory privacy protection method based on information entropy suppression. Comput. Appl. **38**(11), 3252–3257 (2018)
12. Jie, W., Chunru, W., Jianfeng, M., Hongtao, L.: False location selection algorithm based on location semantics and query probability. J. Commun. **41**(03), 53–61 (2020)
13. Hu, Z., Yang, J., Zhang, J.: Trajectory privacy protection method based on the time interval divided. Comput. Secur. **77**, 488–499 (2018)
14. Li, J., et al.: Mobile location privacy-preserving algorithm based on PSO optimization. J. Comput. Sci. **41**(5), 1037–1051 (2018)
15. Pan, J., Liu, Y., Zhang, W.: Detection of dummy trajectories using convolutional neural networks. Secur. Commun. Netw. **2019**, 8431074 (2019)
16. Zheng, H., Xiaofeng, M.: A trajectory data publishing method satisfying differential privacy. J. Comput. Sci. **41**(02), 400–412 (2018)

17. Yin, C., Xi, J., Sun, R., Wang, J.: Location privacy protection based on differential privacy strategy for big data in industrial internet of things. IEEE Trans. Industr. Inf. **14**(8), 3628–3636 (2017)
18. Yan, Y., Gao, X., Mahmood, A., Feng, T., Xie, P.: Differential private spatial decomposition and location publishing based on unbalanced quadtree partition algorithm. IEEE Access **8**, 104775–104787 (2020)
19. Zhao, Y., et al.: Local differential privacy-based federated learning for internet of things. IEEE Internet Things J. **8**(11), 8836–8853 (2020)
20. Tian Feng, W., Laifeng, Z.L., Hai, L., Xiaolin, G.: A personalized differential privacy protection mechanism for trajectory data distribution. J. Comput. Sci. **44**(04), 709–723 (2021)
21. Dwork, C.: Differential privacy. In: Proceedings of the 33rd International Colloquium on Automata, Languages and Programming (ICALP), pp. 1–12. Venice, Italy (2006)
22. Dwork, C., McSherry, F., Nissim, K., Smith, A.: Calibrating noise to sensitivity in private data analysis. In: Halevi, S., Rabin, T. (eds.) TCC 2006. LNCS, vol. 3876, pp. 265–284. Springer, Heidelberg (2006). https://doi.org/10.1007/11681878_14
23. McSherry, F., Talwar, K.: Mechanism design via differential privacy. In: Proceedings of the 48th Annual IEEE Symposium on Foundations of Computer Science (FOCS), pp. 94–103. Providence, RI, USA (2007)
24. Kalman, R.E.: A new approach to linear filtering and prediction problems. J. Basic Eng. **82**, 35–45 (1960)
25. Liyue, F., Xiong, L.: Real-time aggregate monitoring with differential privacy. In: Proceedings of the 21st ACM International Conference on Information and knowledge management, pp. 2169–2173 (2012)
26. Fan, L., Li, X.: An adaptive approach to real-time aggregate monitoring with differential privacy. IEEE Trans. Knowl. Data Eng. **26**(9), 2094–2106 (2014)
27. Datatang. Social network users access geographic location data. http://www.datatang.com/data/43896. 27 Nov 2015

Big Data Grave Register Information Management System Outside Cemeteries Under Internet of Things

Xiu Wen Ye, Yuan Yuan Pan, Yu Yan Peng, GuiQing Tan, and GinQing Tan[✉]

School of Politics and Law, Yulin Normal University, Yulin 537000, Guangxi, China
2011439781@qq.com

Abstract. This article mainly aims at the cemetery outside the tomb positioning, MuZhuRen information collection difficult, compensation difficult problem, the government imposed using unmanned aerial vehicle (UAV) advanced positioning technology, control technology and the key technology of Internet of things – information collection and remote transmission technology and information technology such as collecting cemetery outside the tomb of the digital information, and statistical data to construct cemetery outside the tomb letter grave interest rate management system. So as to build a tomb information management system outside public cemeteries with statistical data. The research findings of this paper can construct a refined three-dimensional model for the high-resolution tomb images taken by UAV aerial photography technology and the specific data obtained by UAV aerial photogrammetry technology. The innovation of this paper is that the information collected by UAVs is transmitted to the mobile phone in real time, which is convenient for the government, cemetery managers and their family members to master the cemetery information. In this paper, through the literature analysis and data analysis of the research methods to build a tomb outside public cemeteries information management system.

Keywords: Big data · Tomb information management system · Unmanned aerial vehicle · Internet of Things

1 Introduction

Nowadays, with the rapid development of society, science and technology lead the trend, and the communication between people is getting closer and closer. As a product of the high-tech era, big data is derived, "From the application level of understanding, the Internet of things refers to all the objects in the world are connected to a network, the formation of "Internet of things", and "Internet of things" and combined with the existing Internet, realizes the human society and the integration of the physical system, achieve more delicate and dynamic management of production and life "(Zhang 2010). "The Internet, telecommunication network and broadcasting network are the basis for the realization and development of the Internet of Things, and the Internet of Things is an

Y.-B. Lin et al. (Eds.): SGIoT 2021, LNICST 447, pp. 128–137, 2022.
https://doi.org/10.1007/978-3-031-20398-5_11

extension and expansion based on the three networks" (Qian and Wang 2012). Internet of Things technology is composed of sensor network, radio frequency tag reading device, bar code and two-dimensional code and other equipment. It is mainly applied in energy, broadband and medical treatment, while big data is mainly applied in genomics, military investigation, finance and medical treatment. This paper aims to build an information management system of tombs outside public cemeteries through big data. Due to the lack of unified management of tombs outside public cemeteries, some tombs are old and have been exposed to the wind and rain for a long time, resulting in blurred information such as tombs and tombstones, and even unknown unowned tombs. From the perspective of geographical location, the tombs outside public cemeteries are not only built on hills and other places, but also built on both sides of the main road, water sources and scenic spots. In the long run, digging for them may result in the collapse of subgrade, river dam and destruction of resources, thus causing incalculable losses. Based on the above reasons, it is necessary to collect the information of the tombs outside public cemeteries and construct the information management system of the tombs outside public cemeteries, which is beneficial to the management of the tombs outside public cemeteries. Due to the advantages of low cost, high surveying and mapping accuracy and wide application range, UAV aerial survey technology has been involved in forestry, land and resources survey, disaster information management, cadastral change and other fields, and its completion degree is high, so UAV is chosen to collect digital information of tombs outside public cemeteries. In order to better manage the tombs outside public cemeteries and maximize the use of land resources, it is necessary to build an information management system of tombs outside public cemeteries.

2 Literature Review

"The Internet of Things (IoT) is the underpinning of its technology. Internet of Things is the extension and application expansion of the Internet, which can realize the information interaction and connection between things and things, and between things and network" (Meng 2018). Therefore, the Internet of Things is closely related to the information management system technology in the context of big data. Management Information System originated in the United States in the late 1960s, and the word "management information system" became popular in 1968" (Wang 2007). In the 1980s, with the emergence of PC (personal computer), information management systems have been really developed, and they have been gradually introduced into China with the rapid progress of network technology. "In the second half of 1980s, the management information system was first applied to Financial software in China in the late 1980s with great success, and then it led to the development of other modules and made outstanding contributions to the management modernization of China" (Yu 2003). With the rapid development of global economy and the improvement of technology, people are welcoming the era of big data with Internet as a typical example, so "information management system" has a more mature explanation: "MIS is a system that takes people as the leading factor and uses computer hardware, software, network communication equipment and other office equipment to collect, transmit, process, store, update and maintain information" (Zhang and Lin 2011). However, what is big data? "Big data is the link that integrates the physical world, information space and human society" (Cheng et al. 2014). It is not difficult to find that big data is the man-machine integration of information collection and processing through computer, Internet, GIS, PS and other technologies, which was born to serve and facilitate human life.

The application of management information system by human beings involves all aspects and covers all fields. For example, in forestry, "GIS technology is used to manage forest resources of collective forests in southern mountainous areas of China, so as to obtain forest information sources timely and accurately for forestry managers and realize resource allocation and structure optimization" (Feng et al. 2001). Another example is the medical level, "Internet network technology is used to integrate the logistics management of medical high-value consumables and the information management of hospital equipment" (Yu and Yu 2006). In order to ensure the timely supply and safety of medical equipment, it also improves the cost performance and reduces the transportation cost. Another example is in the police resources, drug crime because of multiple factors to obtain drug-related intelligence is difficult, based on this public security border drug case intelligence information management system came into being. "Through the computer network management of drug case intelligence information, it can strengthen the collection, management and exchange of drug crime intelligence information in border security departments, and greatly improve the quality of border law enforcement" (Li 2015). Through the above examples, it is obvious that management information systems have been applied in many fields such as agriculture, medicine, law enforcement and othes, and have played an important role in our lives. However, most of the above management information systems adopt a single technical model, which is difficult to popularize all levels of society. Just like with the changes of the times, the burial governance outside public cemeteries has been widely concerned. For example, Article 14 of the Funeral Management Regulations of Guangxi Zhuang Autonomous Region was revised in 2021, and cremation was gradually implemented in areas with burial in the ground. Rural public welfare cemeteries can be set up in townships, towns and villages, and barren hills can be designated in remote mountainous areas to bury remains. It is advocated and encouraged to bury the remains without leaving tombs. It can be seen that some areas attach great importance to the management of tombs outside public cemeteries. At present, a perfect tomb information management system has not been established. Therefore, the author proposes that the establishment of a big data tomb management information system has high research and scientific value. However, how to establish the tomb management information system? Under the background of big data, "through the existing GPS satellite positioning and longitude and latitude coordinates, the specific location of the tomb can be accurately located, and with the help of on-site investigation and image collection, the relevant tomb information can be obtained in detail" (Ye et al. 2017). GPS satellite is used to locate the accurate position, and aerial modeling of UAV can calculate the tomb area after post-technical processing, which provides a basis for future government compensation. On the one hand, the establishment of Tomb Management Information System fills the loopholes in the field of funeral management information system, on the other hand, it is also conducive to efficiently, accurately and effectively alleviating the unreasonable burial phenomenon outside public cemeteries, facilitating the management of government departments and improving their work efficiency.

3 The Analysis of Tomb Information Management System Through Big Data

3.1 Data Collection of Tomb Information Management System

The tomb information management system of tombs outside public cemeteries is beneficial to the scientific management of tombs outside public cemeteries, but the construction of big data information management system needs to consider many factors comprehensively. However, the difficulties in the process of building the system lie in the determination of the location of the cemetery, how to measure the area of the cemetery, how to solve the unknown tomb encountered in the process of confirming the identity of the tomb owner, the address of the tomb owner before his death and the distance between the address and the cemetery. In view of these difficulties, what methods should be used to collect data? Currently, ecological cemeteries in China adopt GPS Position System, Management of cemeteries, while predecessors (Ye et al. 2017) also used GPS (Global Position System) and Satellite Positioning (see Fig. 1) when studying tombs outside public cemeteries. However, satellite positioning is limited by distance, weather, cloud cover and other factors, unless military satellites, it is difficult to take clear photos of cemeteries. The big data tomb information management system adopts UAV aerial survey. (Nan 2020) "UAV aerial survey can adopt UAV platform with multi-rotor and fixed wing, camera sensor equipped with single lens and multi-lens, small airborne radar and others, which is an advanced surveying and mapping technology for UAV survey". (Xu 2020) "UAV technology has the advantages such as flexibility, quick response, high resolution and wide range", and UAV aerial photography can generate a three-dimensional model for the cemetery, and accurately and stereoscopically display the location and morphology of the cemetery. However, the operation of UAV has professional requirements. Therefore, professional operators are needed to adjust the flight height according to the topography of the cemetery and the height of the crown on the basis of the suitable safe flight distance of the UAV. If the crown is blocked, the oblique shooting method can be adopted, and the area of the cemetery can be output according to the whole picture and the shape of the cemetery.

For the way of collecting the identity information related to the tomb owner in the tomb information management system. Ye et al. (2017) put forward that "the identity information of the tomb owner can be collected by means of on-site investigation images", and the information data of the tomb owner can be uniformly entered. However, if the identity information of the tomb owner is entered manually one by one, it is complicated and error-prone. Lin et al. (1998) said, "The existing business card omnipotent king can use smart phones to take business card images, quickly scan business card information and enter them into the system software". The collection of tombstone information can be transformed into the function of tombstone information collection by imitating the business card function, so that the tomb information collectors only need to use smart

Fig. 1. Satellite map of tombs outside Daluoshan Cemetery in Wenzhou City. Data source: Investigation and survey by the team led by the researcher (photo taken on November 6, 2016)

phones to shoot tombstone information in the cemetery, and by shooting tombstones, the automatic entry of tomb information can be realized. Because some cemeteries were built for a long time, or the address of the descendants of the tomb owner is unknown, it is difficult to identify the tombstone information such as the name of the tomb owner, the date of tomstoning and the living address, so the relevant data can be collected by questionnaire survey in the surrounding areas, but some surrounding residents are newly moved residents, or because of their long history, the residents who know the information of the tomb owner have passed away and cannot be investigated. However, China has the custom of sweeping tomb and offering sacrifices in Tomb-Sweeping Day, so the identity information and address of the tomb owners and their descendants can be collected in Tomb-Sweeping Day. In addition, in the tomb information management system, the location of the tomb and the living address of the tomb owner, or the address of the descendants of the tomb owner can be added. In this way, through the distance formula between two points, the shortest distance between the cemetery and the address of the deceased or the descendants of the tomb owner can be calculated, and the radiation range of people building tombs here can be calculated as the diameter, so as to facilitate the government to grasp people's wishes to build cemeteries, thus determining the management scope and saving the budget amount of cemetery management and education and publicity.

3.2 Data Analysis of Tomb Information Management System

It is necessary to analyze the data of the information management system of tombs outside public cemeteries for building a scientific and reasonable information management system of tombs. Among them, the name of the tomb owner, the name and contact information of the descendants of the tomb owner are conducive to confirming the identity of the tomb owner and the kinship of the descendants, and provide subject information for the government to carry out expropriation compensation for legal cemeteries in different periods or the cost of dismantling illegal cemeteries. The living address of the tomb owner helps the government to communicate with the descendants of the tomb owner in time when managing the cemetery; the tomstoning season is conducive to catering to the concept and customs of the descendants of the tomb owner who pay attention to the time of erecting monuments and the choice of feng shui days; The tomstoning time is conducive to the government's legal management of cemeteries according to funeral laws and land management regulations in different periods; The latitude and longitude of the cemetery is beneficial for the descendants of the tomb owner, managers and the government to accurately find the location of the cemetery; Altitude is conducive to understanding the height of the cemetery; Photos around the tomb are convenient for the government to understand the surrounding situation of the cemetery, discover, manage and dismantle illegally built cemeteries in time, and also help the government to master the number of illegally built cemeteries, provide data reference for the government to publicize and educate the information management outside public cemeteries in the surrounding areas, and avoid the waste of human and financial resources; UAV shooting modeling is conducive to showing the whole picture of the cemetery in three dimensions; Shooting time is beneficial for the data collectors of tomb information to master the time of data collection, and take this time as the starting time point to update the tomb data information regularly.

3.2.1 Type of Tomb

Tombs are divided into five types: personal tomb, joint burial tomb, unknown, tomb before death, joint burial tomb + tomb before death (see Fig. 2). Personal tomb refers to the tomb where only one tomb owner is buried; Joint burial tomb refers to the tomb where two dead people are buried; Unknown tomb refers to the vague or unspecified information about the name, living address and burial date of the tomb owner on the tombstone; tomb before death refers to a tomb prepared in advance for the elderly with red fonts. Taking Daluo Mountain in Wenzhou as an example, according to the data in the figure, before 2017, the number of tombs in Daluo Mountain in Wenzhou was mostly joint tombs and unknown tombs. The confirmation of tomb types is beneficial for the government and Civil Affairs Bureau to scientifically control the area of tombs outside public cemeteries, and effectively prevent people from occupying land to build tombs on a large scale under the influence of the funeral concept of "magnificent burial".

3.2.2 Legitimate Construction of Tombs

With the aging of our country becoming more and more serious, the mortality rate is gradually rising. In China, burial is widely used, but land resources are limited, so tombs

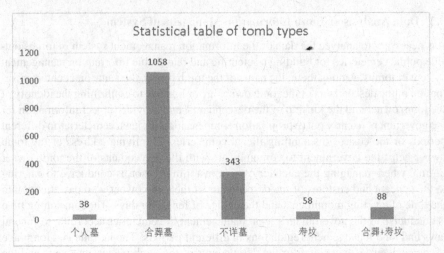

Fig. 2. Number of tomb types. Data source: Investigation and survey by the team led by the researcher

outside public cemeteries should be built according to law. The promulgation of laws and regulations on funeral and interment provides legal basis for the government to manage the construction of tombs outside public cemeteries. Ye et al. (2017) "Funeral management in China can be divided into three stages: from the founding of New China to February 7, 1985, from February 8, 1985, when the Interim Provisions of the State Council on Funeral Management came into effect to July 20, 1997, and from July 21, 1997, when the Regulations on Funeral Management came into effect". According to the survey data of tombs outside Daluoshan Cemetery (see Fig. 3), the number of tombs in this area has continued to increase in different periods. When the government implements the management of tombs outside public cemeteries, it can refer to the funeral laws and regulations of different periods and dismantle illegally built tombs; The cemetery that needs to be expropriated or requisitioned should be coordinated with the descendants of the tomb owner and compensated.

3.2.3 Regular Update of UAV Aerial Photography Data

In some areas of China, there is a funeral custom of "second burial". In this case, it involves the new location, orientation and area change of tombs. At the same time, due to the rising death rate caused by aging in China, many new cemeteries have appeared. Therefore, the data information entered into the system should be modified and updated in time. However, if aerial survey is re-conducted once a month, manpower and material resources will be wasted. Therefore, according to the number of local rebuilt and newly built cemeteries every year, the time of re-aerial survey can be determined to update the system data.

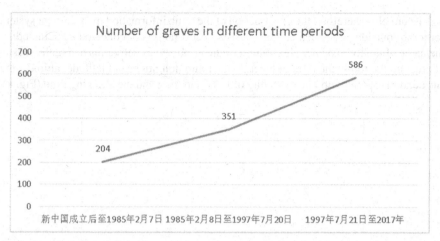

Fig. 3. Number of tombs in different time periods. Data source: Investigation and survey by the team led by the researcher

4 The Construction of Big Data Tomb Information Management System

In order to better manage the tombs outside public cemeteries, it is necessary to build a perfect big data tomb information management system. The big data tomb information management system is combined with modern science and technology, and adopts aerial photography of UAVs to collect data. Although UAV aerial photography has the function of tilting side photography, which avoids the shielding of canopy and bamboo to a certain extent, it is difficult for UAV aerial photography to shoot the whole picture in some cases because some canopy is too high or bamboo is too lush, and the flying height of UAV is limited. Li et al. (2021) "In order to solve the problems of poor GPS signals under the canopy, and the laid control points are easily blocked and can no longer be seen in photos, GPS-PPK technology is used to obtain three relatively accurate line elements (XS, YS, ZS) of the external orientation elements of the photography center at the photography moment, and use them to replace the line elements of the original POS data. On the basis of obtaining the accurate external orientation elements of the photography center by SFM (Structure from Motion) method, DSM is generated by dense matching, and the final result DOM is obtained by manual editing and orthophoto correction. Therefore, the collection of big data can adopt the combination of UAV and PPK technology, so as to build a perfect big data tomb information management system.

In order to facilitate the big data tomb information management system, such as tomb sweeping for descendants of tomb owners, cemetery administrators, relevant staff of Civil Affairs Bureau, etc., to find the cemetery to be searched as soon as possible in the cemetery area, the big data tomb information management system software can be combined with mobile phones. The descendants of the tomb owner sweep the tomb, the cemetery administrator, the relevant staff of the Civil Affairs Bureau, etc., only need to use smart phones to directly enter the tomb information management system, and through detailed analysis of the tomb data information, locate the corresponding cemetery quickly and accurately. Therefore, the construction of the tomb information management system for tombs outside public cemeteries consists of several sets of collected data, including the name of the tomb owner, the address of the tomb owner before his death, the season of erecting the tomb, the time of erecting the tomb, longitude and latitude, altitude, the surrounding of the tomb, the modeling of UAV shooting and the shooting time (Fig. 4).

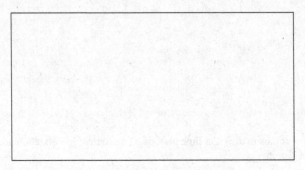

Fig. 4. Data content table. Data source: Self-made by researchers

5   Conclusion

"For a long time, people have completely different views on burial outside public cemeteries. For the descendants of the tomb owner, they think that this is a continuation of the tradition of satisfying the wishes of the deceased and returning to the roots; But for the government, burial outside public cemeteries is a phenomenon that needs to be rectified" (Ye et al. 2017). The remediation method proposed in this paper is to accurately locate the longitude and latitude of tombs outside public cemeteries by using UAV aerial survey technology. The information of tomb owners and their families is obtained by using the unique customs of ancestor worship, family sacrifice and tomb sacrifice in Tomb-Sweeping Day or various regions. On some open hills in rural areas, tombs are often concentrated, so we can use the latitude and longitude of tombs to calculate the distance from cemeteries to nearby villages, so as to determine the management scope of the government. Using the information such as longitude and latitude of cemetery and cemetery area collected by UAVs, a cemetery information management system can be established by using big data technology, which is convenient for cemetery managers and the government to check the cemetery situation in real time. The innovation of this paper lies in the use of UAV shooting technology to establish a tomb information data management system including the information and household registration of the deceased, the information of their close relatives and non-close relatives, the type, area, longitude and latitude of the cemetery, and the tomstoning date of the tomb. The tomb information data management system is connected with the mobile phone, and the UAV aerial survey technology is combined with the geographical vegetation survey technology to establish a three-dimensional model of the tomb outside public cemeteries. And the combination of the Internet of Things and uAVs, "uAV-assisted communication technology of the

Internet of Things, help the Internet of Things to expand the existing network coverage, enhance the flexibility of the Topology of the Internet of Things" (Liu et al. 2020) to help us better collect tomb register information. But how to use UAV shooting and how to use UAV technology to build a refined three-dimensional model, If the technical content of this aspect is perfected, it will save the cost of collection and demolition for the government, effectively reduce the expenditure of government funds, improve the publicity efficiency of the government to the tombs outside public cemeteries, and better realize the land planning.

Acknowledgments. This work was supported by the Research Center for cultural construction and social governance in ethnic areas of Yulin Normal University (2019YJJD0003).

References

Yu, C., Yu, J.: Integrated management of medical high-value consumables logistics and information management system of hospital equipment. J. Manage. Sci. **27**(1), 65–66 (2006)

Wang, T.: Development of management information system. J. Modern Inform. (6), 224–225 (2007)

Feng, X., Song, T., Yao, J., Du, J., Cai, X.: Research and development of collective forest resources information management system based on GIS. J. Beijing For. Univ. **23**(3), 81–85 (2001)

Ye, X., Yang, G., Wang, Y., Zhu, J.: Remediation of burial outside public cemeteries in Daluo Mountain. Wenzhou. Inner Mongolia Scie. Technol. **36**(5), 14–25 (2017)

Li, Y.: Establishment and application of information management system for drug cases in public security border defense. J. Anhui Vocat. Coll. Police Officers **14**(4), 84–86 (2015)

Liu, Y., Dai, H., Wang, Q.J.: J. Internet of Things (4), 48–55 (2020)

Li, Y., Cao, M., Li, C., Yan, F., Feng, Z.: Application of PPK technology in UAV forest aerial photogrammetry. J. Central South Univ. For. Technol. **41**(7), 20–25 (2021)

Zhang, Z., Lin, Y.: Analysis of management information system. Digital Technol. Appl. (4), 157–162 (2011)

Zhang, Y.: Technology and application of Internet of Things. Commun. Inform. Technol. (1), 50–53 (2010)

Meng, X.: Overview of Internet of Things technology. China Sci. Technol. Inform. (23), 46–47 (2018)

Lin, X.-F., Ding, X.-Q., Wu, Y.-S.: Implementation of automatic entry system for business cards. J. Data Acquisition Process. **13**(2), 163–167 (1998)

Yu, L.: The past, present and future of management information system. Guan Li Zong Heng (6), 124–125 (2003)

Nan, Z.: Analysis on the application of UAV aerial survey in land and resources surveying and mapping. Huabei Nat. Res. (4), 102–104 (2020)

Xu, B.: Talking about the application of UAV technology in forestry investigation. South China Agric. **14**(18), 71–72 (2020)

Qian, Z., Wang, Y.: Research on the technology and application of Internet of Things. Acta Electronica Sinica (5), 1023–1029 (2012)

Cheng, X., et al.: Summary of big data system and analysis technology. J. Softw. **9**(25), 1889–1908 (2014)

Critical Feature Selection and Machine Learning-based Models for Monofacial and Bifacial Photovoltaics

Ansari Aadil Shahzad, Prajowal Manandhar, O. A. Qureshi$^{(\boxtimes)}$, Ahmer A. B. Baloch,
Edwin Rodriguez-Ubinas, Vivian Alberts, and Sgouris Sgouridis

Dubai Electricity and Water Authority, Dubai, UAE
{ansari.shahzad,prajowal.manandhar,omer.qureshi,ahmer.baloch,
edwin.ubinas,vivian.alberts,sgouris.sgouridis}@dewa.gov.ae

Abstract. Prediction accuracy has paramount importance in reliable PV solar plant performance. This helps with optimal plant design, economic assessment, smooth grid integration, and plant operations. Machine learning (ML) models help with faster, reliable, and accurate prediction of annual energy yield that is valid over a wide range of climatic conditions, module specifications, and site conditions. In this study, an ensemble-learning algorithm with regression trees is used to predict the performance of both monofacial and bifacial modules. Training data is prepared from parametric simulation results obtained using System Advisor Model (SAM) with an energy yield range of 120–584 kWh/m^2 for monofacial modules and 134–706 kWh/m^2 for bifacial modules. The results showed that ensemble-learning based ML algorithm can predict the energy yield of monofacial and bifacial modules with RMSE of 2.89 kWh/m^2 and 4.65kWh/m^2.

Keywords: Generic Model · Machine Learning · Photovoltaics · Monofacial · Bifacial

1 Introduction

Photovoltaic (PV) cell technology aggressively competes with other renewable technologies based on the lower installation cost and faster return on investment [1]. Monofacial technology has been dominant in the past; however, a new technology that can generate power on both sides of the PV module shows great promise. The market share of bifacial PV cells, modules, and systems offers a pathway to significantly decrease the Levelized cost of energy (LCOE) compared with conventional monofacial PV modules. As a result, bifacial PV technologies are expected to reach 80% of the market share by 2031 [2]. One major barrier to the broader use of bifacial PV modules and systems is a lack of knowledge and experience with a system design that takes advantage of the specific features of bifacial cells. Bifacial system performance cannot be predicted with confidence using current PV performance modeling applications because of difficulties in accurately estimating the reflected irradiance to the back-side. It is therefore crucial

Y.-B. Lin et al. (Eds.): SGIoT 2021, LNICST 447, pp. 138–150, 2022.
https://doi.org/10.1007/978-3-031-20398-5_12

to develop new improve methods to forecast the energy yield (EY) of PV modules to determine the best economic design for a PV solar plant.

Simulation software such as System Advisor Model (SAM), PVSyst, and HelioScope can predict the performance of both monofacial and bifacial modules for different configurations and climates. Fixed modules with a tilt the same as the location's latitude are the most commonly adopted configuration for PV modules in large to small-scale applications. The mentioned simulation software can predict energy yield for this configuration at multiple locations, range of module specifications, and site conditions. However, it's a time-consuming affair and requires careful setup of the software parameters. A trained Machine Learning (ML) based model can be used to predict a PV plant's energy yield with a high accuracy level. These ML models provide the advantage of fast setup and accuracy of the prediction. Accurate and reliable prediction of the power output of other renewable energy sources such as wind turbines using ML models was demonstrated by the previous research [3]. Similar efforts were made to predict the daily mean solar power using ML techniques [4]. However, the prediction of these ML models depends on the training data [5]. Hence, the simulation environment must be set up carefully to obtain the training data for the ML model. Khandakar et al.demonstrated the performance of multiple ML algorithms for predicting the power output of the PV modules operating in Qatar [6]. They could predict the instantaneous output power of a PV module with a minimal RMSE of 2.14 W..

In this work, SAM software is utilized to obtain the annual energy yield of both monofacial and bifacial modules for a wide range of site conditions, module specifications, and climatic conditions. It is observed that an ensemble-learning algorithm with bagged trees can predict the annual energy yield of both PV technologies faster and more accurately. These fast results obtained from ML models can help to perform quick assessments and obtain the near-optimal design of PV plants according to site conditions [4].Also, it can be helpful to estimate the impact of selecting the PV module specifications on plant EY based. Critical feature selection criterion has been determined in this work as well. The selection of the independent variables is performed based on the ranking of the correlation of each independent variable to the dependent variable, which determines their significance to dependent variables such as DC Energy. The correlation of each independent variable to the dependent variable is obtained, and features are selected based on the higher ranks of their correlations. This work aims to incorporate a machine learning approach with simulated data to provide a fast and accurate global estimation of PV module performance.

2 Methodology

This section describes the approach adopted to generate training data, feature selection criteria and development of the ML model. Mainly there are two stages in this process.The training data is generated using the SAM software in the first stage. The range of parametric study is defined to cover a wide range of site conditions and module specifications, followed by a selection of locations to provide global coverage of climatic conditions. This data provides the performance of a fixed-mounted PV module, tilted at an angle the same as the location's latitude, over a wide range of climatic conditions, cell efficiency (η),albedo(α_{sur}), bifaciality (φ_{bi}), and temperature coefficient (γ).

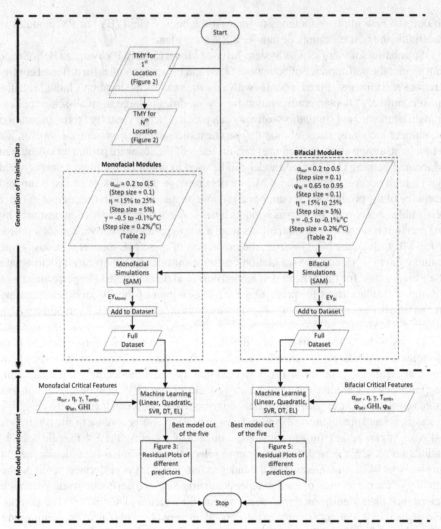

Fig. 1. Pictorial representation of the workflow for the SAM simulations and Machine Learning modeling.

The second stage starts with feature selection by checking the correlation between the parametric study variables and annual energy yield. Once the critical features are selected, multiple ML algorithms are tested and the best-performing algorithm is reported along with the ranking of modeling features. These ML algorithms include Robust linear, Quadratic, Support Vector Regression, Decision Trees and Ensemble Learning. Figure 1 shows the workflow from training data generated from the parametric study to the developing ML models.

2.1 Simulations Model Details

Simple efficiency model is setup in SAM to perform the parametric simulation runs over a wide range of conditions. A standard PV plant with two rows of seven modules, each with a total module area of 10.4 m^2 was set up for the simulations. The modules are oriented in the south direction for locations in the northern hemisphere and vice versa. Modules are tilted at an angle equal to the latitude of that location. Table 1 shows the fixed parameter values of both monofacial and bifacial simulations.

Table 1. Selected values of the parameter in the Simple Efficiency PV model in SAM.

Parameter	Monofacial module	Bifacial module
Module area (A_m)	0.7474 m^2	
Maximum power voltage (V_{mp})	30 V_{dc}	
Open circuit voltage (V_{oc})	36 V_{dc}	
Module structure/Mounting	Glass-cell-glass/Ground mounted	
Module elevation	1.5 m	
Ground coverage ratio	0.3	
Shading	No Shading	
Transmission factor	–	0.013

2.2 Range of Parameters

Table 2 provides the range of parametric studies covered for both monofacial and bifacial simulations. The range of module specifications, such as power temperature coefficient, cell efficiency, and bifaciality, are fully covered in the parametric study, along with a range of possible site albedo. Other site conditions such as GHI and ambient temperature are covered by simulating a wide range of climatic conditions.

Table 2. Summary of parametric study with a range of critical variables

Parameter range	Monofacial simulation	Bifacial simulation
Power temperature coefficient (γ)	−0.5 to −0.1%/°C (Step size = 0.2%/°C)	
Cell efficiency (η)	10%–20% (Step Size = 5%)	
Albedo (α_{sur})	0.2–0.5 [7] (Step size = 0.1)	0.2–0.5 [7] (Step size = 0.1)
Bifaciality (φ_{Bi})	–	0.65–0.95 [8] (Step size = 0.1)

2.3 Selection of Locations

A selected weather station from a grid of $10° \times 10°$ (Latitude $\times$ Longitude) is used as a representative weather station that provides a total of 218 weather stations [9]. Polar or near-polar locations have a very cold climate and low GHI. Hence locations above the latitude of $60°$ and below $-60°$ were removed before random selection. The filtered locations are plotted on the world map with climate classification by Koppen-Geiger [10], as shown in Fig. 2.

Average sun-hours ambient temperature (T_{ASHAT}) was calculated for each location using the subset of hourly temperatures observed during sun-hours. This averaged value should provide a better sense of change in the performance of PV modules compared to the average ambient temperature estimated for all hours throughout the day.

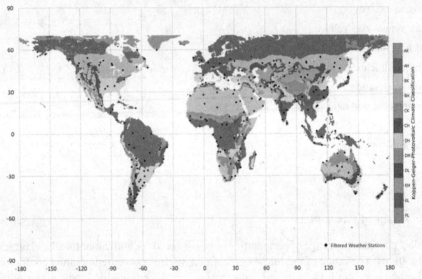

Fig. 2. Koppen-Geiger PV classification w.r.t Irradiation and Temperature. The first letter shows the Temperature-Precipitation zones (A- Tropical, B- Desert, C- Steppe, D- Temperate, E- Cold & F-Polar). The second letter shows the Irradiation zones (K- Very High, H- High, M- Medium & L- Low) [9, 10]

2.4 Feature Selection

The feature selection process allows the identification of significant features constituting the given data. Thus, it facilitates identifying and isolating prominent features to ensure quality in the underlying information. In addition, feature selection reduces the dimensionality of available data, making mining tasks much simpler. In this study, Correlation Ranker-based feature selection algorithm was used to evaluate the features and a rank-list was generated based on their score. These scores were used to select the most relevant features among cell efficiency, albedo, temperature coefficient, bifaciality, irradiance, Average sun-hours ambient temperature, and latitude.

2.5 Machine Learning Model

In this study different ML models have been used to provide an improved prediction of the significant impact of the predictors on the energy yield between bifacial and monofacial modules. These different ML models are compared with robust linear and quadratic models to determine which one of the two PV technologies is affected more by different predictors [11].

Data is key to any black-box model, and there is never enough data to train these model. The full dataset is divided into training and testing datasets in 7:3 ratios in random order. Therefore, removing a part of training data from an already reduced dataset for validation poses a problem of under-fitting. Since the holdout approach reduces the training data size, there is a risk of losing important patterns/trends in the data set, increasing errors induced by bias. Therefore, using the K-fold cross-validation approach in the training dataset that provides ample data for training the model and leaves a subset for validation. In K-fold cross-validation, the data is divided into K-subsets. In the holdout method, the '1/K' part of the data is repeated 'K' times, such that each time, one of the 'K' subsets is used as the validation set and the other 'K-1' subsets are put together to form a training set. The error estimation is averaged over all 'K' trials to get the total effectiveness of the model. In the case of every data, the point gets to be in a validation set exactly once and gets to be in a training set 'K-1' times. This allows to significantly reduce a bias as most of the data is used for fitting, and it also significantly reduces variances as most of the data is also being used for invalidation. And interchanging the training and validation sets also adds to the effectiveness of this method. As a general rule or empirical evidence, $K = 5$ is used in ML modeling.

2.5.1 Support Vector Regression (SVR)

Support Vector Regression (SVR) is a supervised learning algorithm that uses the same principle as the Support Vector Machines (SVM) to model and predicts discrete values [12]. The basic idea behind SVR is to find the best fit line, which is to have the hyperplane that contains the maximum number of points. In SVR, the kernel is used to represent the function to approximate the data. Amongst various kernels available, Gaussian functions (radial basis [15] perform well for the data that shows Gaussian or normal distribution.

2.5.2 Decision Trees (DT)

Decision Trees (DT) is a supervised learning algorithm to predict discrete values of the parameters used to train the model [13]. DT starts at the root and traverses slowly towards the nodes by partitioning the predictors using the divide and conquer strategy as per that predictor that has the highest impact on uniformity in the result after a supervised learning technique used to combine the multiple regression as per the split.

2.5.3 Ensemble Learning (EL)

Ensemble Learning (EL) is a supervised learning algorithm that combines the outputs from various ML approaches, such as decision trees (with various bagging and/or boosting) or various ML models into one [14]. It is primarily used to improve the performance of the regressive prediction or function approximation as ensemble methods use multiple learning approaches to obtain better predictive performance than that could be obtained from any of its constituent learning algorithms alone. In the ensemble approach, 200 bagged trees have been considered and it consist of varying sample of training data.

3 Results and Discussion

Different machine learning models are used to understand the importance of other predictors such as efficiency (η), albedo (α_{sur}), temperature coefficient (γ), bifaciality (φ_{bi}), GHI$_T$, T$_{ASHAT}$, and latitude (φ_{lat}) on the predictors' energy yield of monofacial and bifacial modules.

Table 3 shows that efficiency, GHI, and T$_{ASHAT}$ are the most significant attributes to the dependent variable DC energy yield compared to other attributes for both Monofacial and Bifacial modules. Similarly, latitude has an inverse effect on the EY of the monofacial modules, which means that the higher the absolute value of latitude lower will be the EY. In the case of monofacial modules, the albedo has the least significant attribute. This is expected as the site albedo has very little effect on the EY of monofacial modules compared to bifacial modules, which play an imperative role in predicting performance. For the bifacial module, bifaciality has the least significant attribute. Generally, bifaciality has a higher effect on the performance of vertically oriented bifacial modules [16]. Since, the tilt of the modules was set according to the latitude, the overall effect of change in bifaciality might be diminished. Hence, these two attributes have been removed on separate occasions to see the impact on the prediction performance of each model (see Table 4).

Table 3. Correlation of features to predict EY of Monofacial and Bifacial modules.

Attributes	Monofacial modules	Bifacial modules
Efficiency (η)	0.7716	0.7616
GHI	0.5603	0.5561
T$_{ASHAT}$	0.3325	0.3402
Temperature Coefficient (γ)	0.0912	0.1047
Albedo (α_{sur})	**0.0254**	0.1563
Latitude (φ_{lat})	−0.2302	−0.2336
Bifaciality (φ_{bi})	–	**0.0645**

Table 4 compares RMSE for different machine learning approaches: Support vector regression, decision trees, and ensemble learning along with the robust linear and quadratic model. The R-squared values are given only for the best model out of the above-mentioned models. "Table 4 also shows the change in RMSE when feature with least correlation is removed from their respective model." E.g., removing albedo from the monofacial model results in an increase in RMSE by minimal (<10%) for each of the ML modelling approaches. However, removing bifaciality from bifacial modules can increase the RMSE by as high as 70% compared to the model that includes all the features. Also, there is a notable change in the model correlation due to the exclusion of bifaciality. Physical interpretation, however, supports the inclusion of all these features, so it is recommended to use the model with all features included.

SVR in comparison to statistical models (linear/quadratic) performs better as it uses feature space to transform and fit the data into a higher dimension by using its kernels.

Table 4. Comparison of Root Mean Square Error (RMSE) between different machine learning techniques.

Technology	RMSE (kWh/m^2)					R-squared
	Robust linear	Quadratic	SVR	Decision trees	Ensemble model	
Monofacial model inclusive of all predictors	18.58	7.12	6.63	5.39	2.89	0.998
Monofacial model without albedo	20.06	7.81	6.55	5.59	3.18	0.997
% change in RMSE	*8%*	*10%*	*−1%*	*4%*	*10%*	
Bifacial model inclusive of all predictors	20.61	7.56	6.38	9.85	4.64	0.997
Bifacial model without Bifaciality	22.73	10.65	9.05	10.45	7.89	0.992
% change in RMSE	*10%*	*41%*	*42%*	*6%*	*70%*	

Figure 3 provides details about residual plots for different predictors for monofacial modules. It can be observed that there is no biasness occurring and no specific structure can be observed in the plots.

Figure 4 shows the simulated vs the ensemble modeled response for the DC energy for monofacial modules. It is clear the the response falls between the 5% error for the complete range throughout the prediction and most of the time, the data points are very

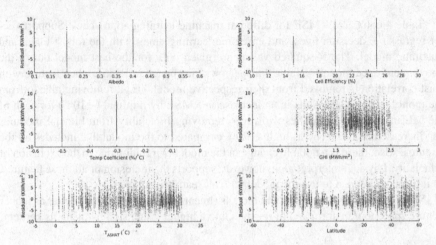

Fig. 3. Residual plots for monofacial modules for all parametric variables to test for any biased error trend (a) w.r.t albedo (b) w.r.t cell efficiency (c) w.r.t. power temperature coefficient (d) w.r.t. aggregate irradiance (e) w.r.t T_{ASHAT} and (f) w.r.t. latitude

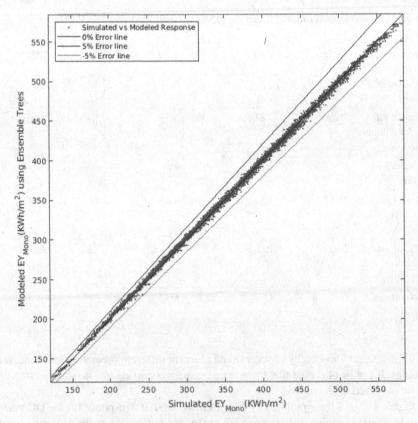

Fig. 4. Prediction performance of ensemble model for monofacial modules

close to the 0% error line. This is because the predicted values of EY are very close to the actual EY generated from the SAM simulations. This shows that the developed ML model model works very accurately.

Figure 5 provides details about residual plots for different predictors for bifacial modules. We can observe that there is no biasness occurring and no specific structure can be observed in the plots.

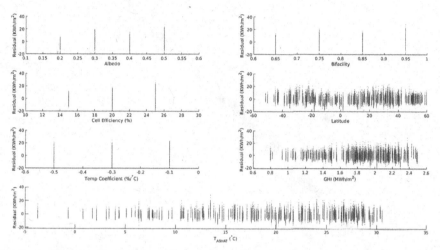

Fig. 5. Residual plots for bifacial modules for all parametric variables to test for any biased error trend (a) w.r.t albedo (b) w.r.t bifaciality (c) w.r.t cell efficiency (d) w.r.t. latitude (e) w.r.t. power temperature coefficient (f) Aggregate Irradiance and (g) w.r.t T_{ASHAT}

Figure 6 shows the simulated vs the ensemble modeled response for the DC energy for bifacial modules. It can be observed that the reposne falls between the 5% error for the complete range throughout the prediction. Since the factors affecting the EY of bifacial modules are comparatively higher than that of monofacial modules, the deviation of data points from the 0% error line increases compared to the monofacial module response.

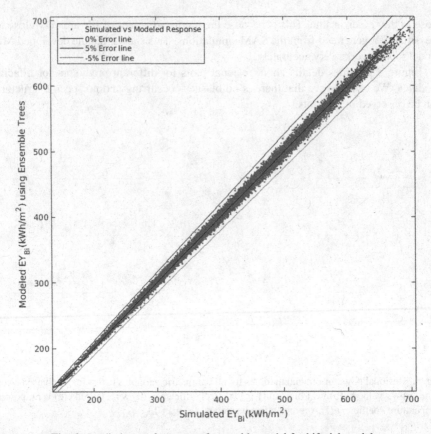

Fig. 6. Prediction performance of ensemble model for bifacial modules.

4 Conclusion

A simulation-based parametric study for both monofacial and bifacial modules was carried out for global climatic conditions. The generated simulation data is used to train and comapre different ML algorithms. Feature selection was done using a correlation ranking filter that allowed choosing significant predictor attributes for DC Energy. Among the analyzed algorithms, ensemble-learning algorithm with bagged trees performed best (RMSE$_{Mono}$= 2.89 kWh/m^2, R$^2_{Mono}$ = 0.9984; RMSE$_{Bi}$ = 4.64 kWh/m^2, R$^2_{Bi}$ = 0.9967) in predicting the output power for both PV technologies.

Nomenclature

Abbreviations		Subscripts	
A	Tropical Regions	amb	Ambient
ASHAT	Average Sun-Hours Ambient Temperature	bi	Bifacial

(continued)

(*continued*)

B	Desert Regions	dc	Direct Current
C	Steppe Regions	lat	Latitude
c-Si	Crystalline Silicon	m	Module
D	Temperate Regions	mono	Monofacial
DT	Decision Trees	mp	Maximum Power
E	Cold Regions	oc	Open Circuit
EL	Ensemble Learning	sur	Surface
EY	Energy Yield (kWh)	t	Total
F	Polar Regions	Symbols	
GCR	Ground Coverage Ratio	α_{sur}	Albedo
GHI	Global Horizontal Irradiation (MWh/m^2)	φ_{bi}	Bifaciality (%)
H	Regions with High Irradiance	φ_{lat}	Latitude
I	Current (Amps)	η	Cell efficiency of PV Module (%)
K	Regions with very High Irradiance	γ	Power Temperature Coefficient (%/°C)
L	Regions with Low Irradiance		
M	Regions with Medium Irradiance		
ML	Machine Learning		
PV	Photovoltaic		
SAM	System Advisor Model		
STC	Standard Test Conditions		
SVR	Support Vector Regression		
T	Temperature (°C)		
TMY	Typical Meteorological Year		
V	Voltage (V)		

References

1. Pv, U.S. Arabia, S.: Saudi Arabia's second PV tender draws a world record low bid of $0.0104/kWh, pp. 6–13 (2021)
2. International, T., Roadmap, T.: Bifacial solar cells, and modules. https://pv-manufacturing.org/bifacial-solar-cells-and-modules/ (2020)
3. Mishra, S.P., Dash, P.K.: Short term wind power forecasting using Chebyshev polynomial trained by ridge extreme learning machine. In: 2015 IEEE Power, Communication and Information Technology Conference (PCITC), pp. 173–177 (2015)
4. Jawaid, F., NazirJunejo, K.: Predicting daily mean solar power using machine learning regression techniques. In: 2016 Sixth International Conference on Innovative Computing Technology (INTECH), pp. 355–360 (2016)

5. Sheng, H., Xiao, J., Cheng, Y., Ni, Q., Wang, S.: Short-term solar power forecasting based on weighted gaussian process regression. IEEE Trans. Industr. Electron. **65**(1), 300–308 (2018)
6. Khandakar, A., et al.: Machine learning based photovoltaics (PV) power prediction using different environmental parameters of Qatar. Energies **12**(14), 2782 (2019)
7. Product-updates, P. U. B. Surface Albedo – most frequent questions, pp. 1–12 (2019)
8. Deline, C., et al.: Evaluation and field assessment of bifacial photovoltaic module power rating methodologies. In: 2017 IEEE 44th Photovoltaics Special Conference PVSC 2017, pp. 1–6 (2017)
9. Lawrie, L.K., Crawley, D.B.: Development of global typical meteorological years (TMYx) (2019). https://climate.onebuilding.org/ (Accessed 10 Oct 2021)
10. Ascencio-Vásquez, J., Brecl, K., Topič, M.: Methodology of Köppen-Geiger-Photovoltaic climate classification and implications to a worldwide mapping of PV system performance. Sol. Energy **191**, 672–685 (2019)
11. Su, D., Batzelis, E., Pal, B.: Machine learning algorithms in forecasting of photovoltaic power generation. In: 2019 International Conference on Smart Energy Systems and Technologies (SEST), pp. 1–6 (2019)
12. Drucker, H., Burges, C.J.C., Kaufman, L., Smola, A., Vapnik, V.: Support vector regression machines. In: Proceedings of the 9th International Conference on Neural Information Processing Systems (NIPS'96), pp. 155–161. MIT Press, Cambridge, MA, USA (1996)
13. Safavian, S.R., Landgrebe, D.: A survey of decision tree classifier methodology. IEEE Trans. Syst. Man Cybern. **21**(3), 660–674 (1991)
14. Arbib, M.A.: The Handbook of Brain Theory And Neural Networks (1998)
15. Wu, Y., Wang, H., Zhang, B., Du, K.-L.: Using radial basis function networks for function approximation and classification. Int. Sch. Res. Not. **2012**, 324194 (2012)
16. Baloch, A..A..B.., Hammat, S., Figgis, B., Alharbi, F.H., Tabet, N.: In-field characterization of key performance parameters for bifacial photovoltaic installation in a desert climate. Renew. Energy **159**, 50–63 (2020)

Study on the Discovery of Personal Information on the Network of People Diagnosed with COVID-19

Cheng Yong Liu[1], Xin Yang Pan[2], Hong Xiang Wang[2], Dan Ni Ling[2], and Xiang Tan[2(✉)]

[1] Jimei University, Xiamen, China
[2] School of Politics and Law, Yulin Normal University, Yulin 537000, Guangxi, China
3441719265@qq.com

Abstract. The arbitrary disclosure of information of people diagnosed with COVID-19on the network will adversely affect personal privacy and even violate the privacy rights of individuals. Through the method of literature analysis and case analysis, the information of the confirmed patients of COVID-19 is studied on the network disclosure. The study found that information disclosure can be divided into disclosable information and non-disclosure information, and make different ways of dealing with sensitive information, sensitive information must be handled with care, personal information processing must take into account the balance between personal interests and public interests.

Keyword: COVID-19 Personal Information Protection Privacy

1 Introduction

COVID-19 broke out in early 2020, and until the beginning of October 2021, the cumulative number of confirmed cases was as high as 238,699,648, and the death toll was 4,873,011. The main infection route of COVID-19 is through respiratory droplets and contact, which means that it is a challenge for COVID-19 prevention and control to act arbitrarily for those who have symptoms or asymptomatic diagnosis. At present, in order to effectively prevent the spread of COVID-19, certain information of confirmed patients will be announced on the Internet, so that the public can raise their awareness of prevention and reduce the probability of infection. Which is one of the methods adopted by the Chinese government. On the one hand, if the announced information is too detailed, excessive publication of the information of the confirmed person may cause some harm to the published person, and even make the unspecified person know the identity of the confirmed person, which may infringe on the personal information or privacy of the confirmed person. On the other hand, if the relevant information is not announced, the people will lack vigilance, which may cause a breach in epidemic prevention. In this case, how to protect personal information and privacy while taking into account the epidemic prevention protection of public interests? How to balance the degree and scope

Y.-B. Lin et al. (Eds.): SGIoT 2021, LNICST 447, pp. 151–161, 2022.
https://doi.org/10.1007/978-3-031-20398-5_13

of information disclosure of confirmed patients? To solve the above problems, it is necessary to analyze the specific information content announced by China for COVID-19 patients through big data, and then put forward feasible suggestions while taking into account both public and private interests.

2   Literature Review

The right to privacy is a specific personality right. Privacy refers to the private space, private activities and private information enjoyed by natural persons and unwilling to be known by others. The right to privacy is the right of natural persons to make their own decisions on appealing information. The important content of the right to privacy is to give the subject the right to control to what extent others can intervene in their private life, and to decide whether to disclose their privacy to others and the scope of disclosure. American jurists Lusamore Warren and Ease Brantis put forward the concept of privacy with legal significance, which has a history of 121 years. They first put forward the concept of the right to privacy in the article "The Right to Privacy" published in Harvard Law Review. After that, the right to privacy stepped onto the legal stage. In 2001, the Supreme People's Court's Interpretation on Confirming the Liability for Compensation for Mental Damage in Civil Tort officially recognized the legal status of the right to privacy in civil justice. China passed the Tort Liability Law of the People's Republic of China at the 12th Meeting of the Standing Committee of the 11th National People's Congress on December 26, 2009. This is the first time that China has directly established the legal status of the right to privacy in the field of civil basic law, and raised the protected privacy interests into independent legal rights. This has created a "new right era" for the protection of privacy in China, which is of great significance in the legal construction of China. Li Ming, Yang Lixin and Yao Hui (1997) pointed out in the Law of Personality Rights that the right to privacy came into being at the beginning to oppose the excessive reporting and dissemination of news. Zhang Lu (2021) pointed out that privacy interest is a concrete personal interest, which embodies personal dignity and personal freedom and is an important embodiment of civil law value.

With the increasing penetration of the Internet into various fields of society, the right to privacy has become a basic right, while the virtual nature of the network leads to the privacy protection on the network which is different from the privacy protection in real life. Liu Yijun and Liu Haidong (2010) believe that the effective operation of virtual society depends entirely on the data identified by individuals to distinguish online people and specify each individual in the process, and it is the right to privacy that protects personal data. Therefore, the importance of network privacy is self-evident. However, when the information of COVID-19 patients was exposed, the security of network information was seriously threatened. Wei Daopei (2010) believes that the developed high technology makes the right to privacy easier to disclose. Gao Wenying (2016) believes that if personal data is disseminated on the Internet, it will involve citizens' information security and personal dignity. Liu Ying (2015) pointed out that people's privacy becomes easy to disclose under the background of big data, which may lead to serious consequences. When unnecessary information is published, it may also have unpredictable consequences. Li Zhongxia (2021) pointed out in "Constitutional Construction of Privacy in Digital Age" that whether personal information is private or not, it may bring considerable troubles and burdens to individuals after being fermented by the Internet. To sum up, the disclosure of network information of COVID-19 confirmed patients will lead to the damage of natural person's rights and the emergence of social rumors. Wang Jun (2020) believes that the conflict between the public's right to know and the right to privacy under pandemic is facing a dilemma, and the key reason lies in the lack of legal basis. For the problems caused by information disclosure at this stage, there are great loopholes in the treatment scheme. For the conventional solution, Li Zhongxia (2021) explained in "Constitutional Construction of Privacy in the Digital Age": limiting personal information too narrow to privacy may not be conducive to privacy protection; However, extending privacy over all personal information control may make privacy lose its essential attributes, which is not conducive to the dissemination and exchange of information. Ji Qiong pointed out that sharp conflicts arise when dealing with issues related to satisfying the public's right to know and ensuring the reintegration of socially controversial people.

3   Problem Analysis

3.1   Global Pandemic Situation and Impact Analysis

At present, the global COVID-19 vaccination rate is gradually increasing, but the global pandemic situation is still grim (see Fig. 1). Since the end of December 2019, COVID-19 has caused a total of 241,353,659 confirmed cases and 4,913,085 deaths worldwide, with 26,085,632 confirmed cases (see Fig. 2). The scope of its infection and the depth of its harm are really shocking under the data display. COVID-19 belongs to Class B infectious disease, but it is highly contagious, so it is managed according to Class A infectious disease. Society will require stricter isolation for COVID-19 patients. Therefore, due to the demand of data statistics of COVID-19 patients and anti-epidemic work, the relevant state institutions have strict control over the personal information of COVID-19 patients. The information of COVID-19 patients is still paid attention to by all sectors of society, and a series of controversies about the publication degree of COVID-19 patient information content are gradually increasing. The cases of COVID-19 patients' information flaws are also on the rise, and a series of problems caused by them can not be ignored.

3.2   Analysis of the Current Situation of Disclosure of Personal Information of COVID-19 Patients

With the spread of COVID-19 pandemic, the number of COVID-19 patients is gradually increasing, and the treatment and prevention of COVID-19 pandemic are carried out simultaneously in various countries. In order to complete the authoritative investigation report of the epidemic and provide more accurate and detailed data information, the flow report organizers need to grasp the accuracy of the time and space of the patient's journey and grasp the real data provided by the masses in time. This will help treat patients and track close contacts as soon as possible, and prevent the spread of pandemic. However, in the process of data collection and management, information leakage is inevitable (see

Fig. 1. Statistical chart of existing COVID-19 in the world. **Source**: Fast information, overseas pandemic module[1]

Fig. 3). According to statistics, 60% of respondents have seen the personal information of COVID-19 patients on social platforms, which shows that the phenomenon of personal information leakage of COVID-19 patients often occurs.

The leaked personal information of patients has exceeded the scope of public welfare. The leaked contents in almost all related cases include the patient's real name, age, gender, ID number, telephone number, home address and other personal privacy information. Taking China as an example, searching Baidu with "COVID-19 information leakage" as the key word, we can see that COVID-19 patient information leakage cases have occurred in many provinces and cities in China. At the same time, due to information leakage, COVID-19 patients were blatantly abused and accused by netizens, and inexplicably threatened and intimidated by strangers, resulting in physical and mental injuries that COVID-19 patients could not recover from.

However, when the flow report is published in the public, the patient's true identity is easily insinuated due to the improper publication of the patient's personal information, which brings different degrees of influence, trouble and even indelible harm to the patient. Search in Baidu with "COVID-19 information leakage" and "COVID-19 confirmed case track" as keywords, Screening distinct cases on pages 1 to 6 and 1 to 7 of the web page respectively, The provinces and cities of these cases are suspected of being too detailed about the patient information mentioned in the brief introduction of the announcement documents of COVID-19 patients (see Table 1). For example, the publication of name, age and gender makes it easy for relatives and friends they know to insinuate the true identity of patients, and the detailed home address published at the same time makes it easier for people in the same community or villages and towns to insinuate their identity, causing suspicion and rumors on the Internet, bringing great troubles to the normal life of COVID-19 patients and even causing cyber violence.

---

[1] Public data from the National Health and Health Commission, provincial and municipal health and health commissions, provincial and municipal governments, Hong Kong, Macao and Taiwan official channels, compiled by Fast Information APP.

3.3 Analysis of Information Disclosure of COVID-19 Confirmed Patients

Citizens' personal information refers to all kinds of information recorded electronically or in other ways that can identify the identity of a specific natural person or reflect the activities of a specific natural person alone or in combination with other information, including name, ID number, communication contact information, address, account password, property status, whereabouts and so on. For the information collation

Fig. 2. Global pandemic statistics table. **Source:** UC Browser[2]

[2] Supported by UC browser, it is compiled according to the public information of National Health and Health Commission, provincial and municipal health and health commissions, Hong Kong, Macao and Taiwan and overseas authoritative official channels and media. This chart was extracted from Alipay Global Pandemic Service Module on October 17, 2021.

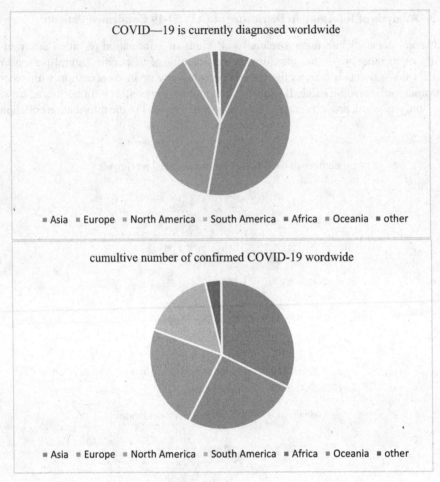

Fig. 2. (*continued*)

and collection of COVID-19 flow report, the patient's personal information has privacy scope.

Since the outbreak of pandemic last year, the disclosure of personal privacy information of COVID-19 patients has aroused continuous concern in the society, and the society has been arguing endlessly about the privacy disclosure caused by the details of the information published in the flow report. According to statistics reported by the media, Since pandemic, there have been at least 20 leaked information incidents involving COVID-19 patients and their relatives in various places, and almost all the leaked information was leaked after the publication of the flow report. Therefore, it is not difficult to speculate that the information leakage occurred during the collection process or the vicious exposure of criminals according to the information published in the report.

According to this, it can be concluded that the contents of COVID-19 patient information published in various provinces and cities are improper between public and private.

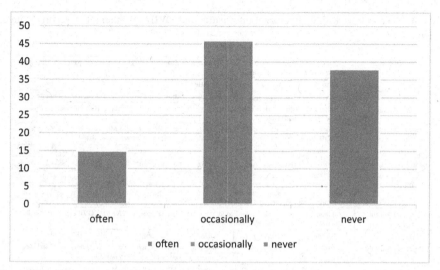

Fig. 3. Statistics on the information status of COVID-19 patients seen by netizens on social platforms. **Source:** Baidu, China Youth Daily (September 23, 2021, titled: Only 500 yuan is fined for leaking the privacy of COVID-19 patients? There are also civil channels to be held accountable)

According to the data collected in the chart (see Table 1), the authoritative patient information should have been prepared for public work such as anti-epidemic and preventing pandemic spread, but the published information is too detailed. For example, if the coding degree of names is low, it is easy to be suspected by netizens and cause rumors, while there is no need to publish the contents of gender, age and detailed home address at the same time, that is, it is not necessary for epidemic prevention work to publish multiple information at the same time. Otherwise, the published content will indirectly reveal the patient's personal privacy information, It will not only run counter to the original intention of publishing information, but also become a tool to infringe on patients' privacy rights, which will cause patients whose information has been leaked to bear undeserved harm and pressure. Therefore, the balance of interests between public rights and private rights in the publication of the flow report of patients and their relatives in epidemic prevention work remains to be solved.

4   Perfection and Suggestions

4.1   Balance Between Public Interests and Private Interests

How to take into account the protection of personal information under the background of pandemic prevention and control deserves attention and consideration.

Generally speaking, in the special period of public safety incidents such as pandemic, the relevant departments need to disclose some information according to law for the purpose of public interest and safety. This involves how to make a "balance" between publishing personal information and protecting public interests, public right to health and right to know. The information that can be disclosed includes: the personal action track of

Table 1. Cases of disclosure of personal information in COVID-19 patient flow report (Source: Baidu)

Published content \ case	Case 1: On December 8, 2020, the information of Zhao, a COVID-19 confirmed patient in Chengdu, Sichuan Province, was leaked.				
Name	Zhao Mou	Gender	Female	Age	20 years old
Provinces and citie	Chengdu, Sichuan	Home address	Chenghua District Cuijiadian Huadu Yunjingtai Community		
Place of stay	Zhongzhi Central Park, Hi Blues Nail Shop, Hepburn Bar, Alley Malatang, Haiwuli Small Bar, play house Wine and other places				
Published content \ case	Case 2: From December 23 to 24, 2020, the information of Yin Moumou, a newly diagnosed COVID-19 patient, and his close contacts in Shenyang, Liaoning Province was leaked.				
Name	Yin Moumou	Gender	Female	Age	67 years old
Provinces and citie	Shenyang, Liaoning	Home address	Shenyang Yuhong District Beiling Neighbourhood Hongda Ji ayuan Community		
Place of stay	On November 29, I arrived at Shenyang Taoxian Airport by CZ682 flight (seat number: 32C) from South Korea. According to the control measures for overseas personnel entering Shenyang, during the centralized isolation period				
Published content \ case	Case 3: On May 9, 2021, after Fan in Yinchuan, Ningxia tested positive for COVID-19 virus, the de tailed flow report was exposed on the Internet.				
Name	Fan Mou	Gender	Male	Age	31 years old
Provinces and citie	Yinchuan, Ningxia	Home address	Xingqing District Nanxun West Street Supply and Marketing Cooperative Family Courtyard Community		
Place of stay	Hedong Airport, Xingqing District Nanxun West Street Supply and Marketing Cooperative Family Courtyard Community, Nanjing Medical University General Hospital Surgical Building and other areas				
Published content \ case	Case 4: On November 19, 2020, Yang's family in Tianjin was diagnosed as a new case of COVID-19, and the information of the flow report was leaked.				
Name	Yang; Yang Moumou (father of Yang); Du Moumou (Mother of Yang)	Gender	Male; Male; Female	Age	35 years old; 61 years old; 59 years old
Provinces and citie	Tianjin	Home address	Building 19, Kanhaixuan Community, Dongjiang Port Area, Tianjin		
Place of stay	TEDA Hospital, Children's Heart Small Yale University of Science and Technology Kindergarten and other related places				
Published content \ case	Case 5: On November 19, 2020, Shenmou, Tianjin was diagnosed as a new case of COVID-19, and the detailed flow report was released.				
Name	Shen Mou	Gender	Male	Age	22 years old
Provinces and citie	Tianjin	Home address	Staff dormitory in a certain district of Shaanxi Road, Binhai New Area, Tianjin		
Place of stay	Tianjin Dongjiang Port Area Kanhaixuan Community, Binhai New Area Shaanxi Road Staff Dormi tory				
Published content \ case	Case 6: On December 7, 2020, there were 2 new confirmed cases of COVID-19 in Chengdu, and the flow report was released.				
Name	Lu Moumou; Zhao Moumou (Lu Moumou's husband)	Gender	Female; Male	Age	69 years old; 71 years old
Provinces and citie	Chengdu, Sichuan	Home address	Group 11, Taiping Village, Pitong Street		
Place of stay	Taiping Village, Pitong Town, People's Hospital of Pidu District, Minyang Middle School of Pidu District, Shaxi Farmers Market and MCC Central Park Community				
Published content \ case	Case 7: On December 8, 2020, there were 3 new confirmed cases of COVID-19 in Chengdu, and the flow report was released.				
Name	Li Moumou; Zhang Moumou	Gender	Female; Female	Age	71 years old; 68 years old
Provinces and citie	Chengdu, Sichuan	Home address	Group 11, Taiping Village, Pitong Street		
Place of stay	A teahouse in Taiping Village, a small clinic in Taiping Village and Xinminchang Town; Taiping Vil lage Vegetable Market, Sandaoyan Town Sanyan Village Resettlement Site				
Published content \ case	Case 8: On November 9, 2020, Shanghai disclosed a new case, and the patient was Wang Moumou, who was engaged in handling work at Pudong Airport.				
Name	Wang Moumou	Gender	Male	Age	51 years old

(continued)

Table 1. (*continued*)

Provinces and citie	Shanghai	Home address	Yingqian Village, Zhenjiang Town Community, Zhuqiao Town, Pudong New Area		
Place of stay	Jiangzhen Baipinhui, Jiangzhen Wanxia Road Food Market, Miaojing Road Social Security Center and other places				
Published content \ case	Case 9: On November 9, 2020, a new close contact of asymptomatic infected person was announced in Tianjin.				
Name	Zhu Moumou	Gender	Male	Age	38 years old
Provinces and citie	Tianjin	Home address	People from Dongdi Village, Duancun Town, Anxin County		
Place of stay	At 16:00 on November 7, 2020, passengers took the bus from Tianjin Jinfulin Market The car (license plate number FF6145) arrived at Dongdi Village Station in Duancun Town, Anxin County at 19:00, Dongdi Village in Duancun Town and Jinfu, Tianjin Forest market				
Published content \ case	Case 10: Lin Mojie and his family, who were hotly debated by public opinion in September 2021, were harassed by cyber violence due to information leakage.				
Name	Lin Mojie	Gender	Male	Age	38 years old
Provinces and citie	Putian, Fujian	Home address	People from Fengting Town, Xianyou County, Putian City		
Place of stay	On August 4th, take Xiamen Airlines Flight 852 from Singapore to Xiamen Airport, and then go to the designated hotel for isolation.				

the parties or patients, close contacts, the communities and places where they have stayed, the people they have contacted, etc. However, the publication of patient information should be cautious. On this premise, the age, sex, occupation, relationship with previous cases, illness, some action tracks and the number of close contacts of patients or suspected infected persons can be disclosed. However, without the consent of the parties concerned, the personal information and privacy of any unit or individual, such as personal name, age, ID card number, telephone number, home address, personal life, personal diary, photo book, savings and property status, living habits, communication secrets and kinship, should not be publicly disclosed. Due to the need of joint prevention and control work, and after desensitization treatment, except. It is suggested that the health system should adjust the publicity of patient information. The most useful information for the masses is the range of patients' activities and behavior track. These contents, together with the flow adjustment and detection of relevant departments, can effectively identify risks. Therefore, I personally believe that the patient's name, gender, age and occupation do not need to be publicized, because for the epidemic prevention department, this information has been understood and no longer needs to be known; For the masses, these patient information is almost useless for personal protection and increases the risk of privacy leakage.

4.2 Improve the System of Personal Privacy Information Disclosure

According to the relevant laws of our country, personal privacy is protected during pandemic. Article 12 of the Law of the People's Republic of China on the Prevention and Control of Infectious Diseases clearly stipulates that "disease prevention and control institutions and medical institutions shall not disclose relevant information and materials involving personal privacy". The Law of the People's Republic of China on Public Security Administration Punishment, the Cyber Security Law of the People's Republic of China and other relevant laws and regulations also have more refined provisions. Recently, all localities and departments have issued documents and notices, requiring information protection during pandemic prevention and control. The Ministry of

Transport issued the Emergency Notice on Coordinating the Prevention and Control of Pandemic and Transportation Security, which requires strict protection of personal privacy and personal information security according to law. Except for providing passenger information to health and other departments due to the need of prevention and control of Pandemic, relevant information shall not be disclosed to other institutions, organizations or individuals, and shall not be disseminated on the Internet without authorization. The Law on the Prevention and Control of Infectious Diseases stipulates that the state should establish a pandemic information disclosure system for infectious diseases, but the scope of information disclosure is not clear, and there is no specific division between compulsory disclosure and optional disclosure, so the practical operation mostly depends on the independent balance of the health administrative department. The author believes that the collection and release of patient information must be directly related to epidemic prevention, and should be closely related to this purpose, and should be set according to the degree of influence of patient personal information on public interests.

The collection of personal information related to pandemic is very important for the prevention and control of COVID-19 pandemic. It is not only a right granted by law, but also a need to perform statutory duties for relevant departments and institutions to collect information according to law. In the process of collection, we should follow the principle of minimum necessity and limit the purpose, that is, the purpose of collecting information is to carry out prevention and control measures such as investigation, inspection, sample collection and isolation treatment of infectious diseases, and information unrelated to pandemic prevention and control cannot be collected. Specific to COVID-19 pandemic prevention and control, the subject who has the right to collect personal information has the right to collect the following information according to the actual needs of pandemic prevention and control:

1. Basic personal information: such as name, ID number, contact information, address and other information;
2. Information related to pandemic prevention and control: such as body temperature, symptoms, relevant residence history, transportation records, relevant contact history and other information. In addition, other personal information unrelated to pandemic prevention and control, such as personal biometric information, network identity information, personal property information, professional information, nationality, religious belief, etc., should not be collected.

As the will of the sovereign and the universal norm of people's behavior, law should be universally observed within its validity period. Under normal circumstances, no organization or individual has the right to collect personal information without consent. Under the background of pandemic prevention and control, for the need of safeguarding social public interests, laws and regulations make exceptions to the collection of personal information, which is already a compromise and reconciliation for the protection of personal information. Because it is a compromise and reconciliation, we should strictly grasp the limits of personal information collection and realize the balance between pandemic information collection and personal information protection.

5 Summarize

For the privacy protection of COVID-19 infected persons, it is very important to correctly and reasonably disclose some privacy of infected persons who meet the current pandemic prevention and control needs on the Internet through literature analysis and case analysis, which can reduce the risk of infection, set obstacles during the transmission, and take into account the protection of personal information privacy. Perfecting the system of personal privacy disclosure is not only a respect for national citizens, but also a protection of social privacy and national information. In-depth research in the process of information generation, screening and dissemination can improve the safety factor of information exchange, reduce the risk of leakage of important national information, and realize a beautiful home together.

References

Wang Liming, F., Yang Lixin, S., Yao Hui, T.: Personality Right Law. Law Press, p. 147 (1997)

Zhang Lu, F.: What is private information? –Based on the discussion of the intersection of privacy and personal information protection in the Civil Code. J. Gansu Univ. Politi. Sci. Law **1**, 93–94 (2021)

Liu Yijun, F., Liu Haidong, S.: "The Legal Application of" Human Flesh Search "Infringing on Others' Privacy and Reputation Rights", "Legal Application", No. 7, 35 (2010)

Wei Daopei, F.: American Privacy Leak Causes Legal Problems. Extraterritorial Legal System 14–15 (2010)

Gao Wenying, F.: On the Protection of Citizens' Information Privacy and Self-determination from Public Security Information Collection, Research on Administrative Law 12–15 (2016)

Ying, L.: The confrontation between spear and shield-research on the current situation of privacy leakage under the background of big data. Rule of Law and Society, next issue in December, 192–193 (2015)

Zhongxia, L.: Constitutional Construction of Privacy in the Digital Age Journal of East China University of Political Science and Law, No. 3, 43-50(2021)

Jun, W.: On the legal balance and protection of the public's right to know and privacy under the governance of major pandemics in the city. Henan Social Sciences Apr. **28**(4), 76–77 (2020)

Qiong, J.: From identity distinction to interest distinction: dilemma and reconstruction of privacy restriction principle in China. J. Gansu Univ. Polit. Sci. Law **1**, 77–79 (2020)

Du Yunyi, F.: How to protect your privacy under the epidemic?Chongqing's first case of COVID-19 infringement civil privacy 1 Yuan, Citizen Guide, 02–07 (2021)

Zhuang Wei, F.: Analysis of the protection of citizens' personal information during the epidemic period, Legal System and Society, 03–15 (2020)

Liu Ran Ran, F., Zheng Zhongwei, S.: Conflict and balance between the privacy of COVID-19 patients and the public's right to know, Decision Exploration, 10–23 (2020)

Wu Wenpin, F.: Legal protection countermeasures of personal information in the epidemic prevention and control. Traffic Construction and Management 06–25 (2020)

Yu Shiqi, F.: Legal protection of data in flow adjustment and tracking, Hebei Law, pp. 10–05 (2020)

Author Index

Printed in the United States
by Baker & Taylor Publisher Services